The Builder's Mindset

Pathway to Money & Success

Ignazio Ibba

ISBN: 978-1-7640006-0-4

Book Cover by Ignazio Ibba

Designed by Red Feather Publishing

www.redfeather.com.au

To fatherhood,

Nobody taught me to be a father, I tried.

Ignazio

Contents

Introduction: The Framework for Unstoppable Success

Success is not inherited, it is built. It is the result of hard work, discipline, and a mindset that turns challenges into opportunities. My story is proof of this. Born and raised in Sardinia, I grew up surrounded by builders; men and women who shaped not just physical structures, but lives of purpose and resilience.

My grandfather, a saddler maker and leather craftsman, taught me the value of precision and patience. My father, a builder, showed me how to turn blueprints into reality, one brick at a time. From them, I learned that building is not just about tools and materials, but vision, effort, and the willingness to keep going, no matter what.

This book is not just my story; it is a practical guide, a step-by-step framework for achieving success. It is the result of decades of trial, error, and hard-earned victories. Whether you're an entrepreneur, a professional, or someone looking to take control of your life, this book will give you the tools to build the future you want.

A Journey Shaped by Adversity, Mentorship, and Education

My path to success was far from easy. I started with little more than determination and a willingness to work harder than anyone else. I faced setbacks that would have broken many a failing marriage, financial struggles, and the constant pressure to provide for my daughter.

But every challenge taught me something valuable.

Two things made all the difference in my journey: mentorship and education.

In the 1990s, I discovered *Millionaire* magazine and books like *The 7 Habits of Highly Effective People* by Stephen R. Covey. These resources opened my eyes to new ways of thinking and gave me the tools to turn my life around. But it was the mentors I met along the way, experienced builders, entrepreneurs, and leaders who showed me how to apply those lessons in the real world.

Mentorship taught me that success is not a solo journey. It's about learning from those who have walked the path before you, avoiding their mistakes, and building on their wisdom. Education, whether through books, courses, or hands-on experience, gave me the knowledge to make smarter decisions and seize opportunities.

A Proven System, Not Just Theory

This is not motivational fluff. This is a proven system that works; the builder's framework.

Across seven sections and 37 chapters, this book gives you a complete, actionable framework for building a powerful life and business. Every part of this journey reflects real foundations, structures, and strategies—just like in construction.

- **Part One: The Foundations**

We begin by laying the emotional and personal groundwork: understanding your past, the power of family, the sacrifices required, and how to turn adversity into purpose.

- **Part Two: The Internal Structure**

This is where you forge your mindset. Vision. Discipline. Self-awareness. You'll discover how to tame fear, strengthen character, and build the mental architecture to support long-term success.

- **Part Three: Practical Tools**

Builders don't just dream they *execute*. You'll learn time management, planning, focus, and how to implement systems that produce daily results. You'll stop being busy and start being effective.

- **Part Four: Relationships and Leadership**

No empire is built alone. You'll master communication, negotiation, and leadership skills. You'll learn how to build solid relationships that support your mission, not distract from it.

- **Part Five: Facing Challenges**

Crises are inevitable. What matters is how you respond. These chapters teach you resilience, adaptation, and how to keep building when everything seems to collapse.

- **Part Six: Expansion and Growth**

With your structure in place, now you scale. These chapters focus on financial control, strategic growth, finding your niche, and building a company culture that lasts.

- **Part Seven: Meaning and Legacy**

True success is not about money alone. It's about *impact*. You'll learn how to give, how to teach, how to build something eternal. Something bigger than yourself.

In the final section, *The 11 Keys of the Builder's Mindset*, I distill all the principles into a set of guiding rules that will keep you grounded, focused, and moving forward, no matter the challenges you face.

The Role of Mentorship and Education

One of the most important lessons I've learned is that no one succeeds alone. Mentors provide guidance, perspective, and accountability. They help you see blind spots, avoid costly mistakes, and stay focused on your goals. Education, whether formal or self-directed, equips you with the knowledge and skills to navigate an ever-changing world.

In this book, I'll share how I sought out mentors, learned from their experiences, and used education as a tool for growth. These elements were crucial to my success, and they can be for yours too.

Who This Book Is For

I'm not an academic or a self-help guru. I'm a builder, someone who has learned through doing. This book is for anyone who refuses to settle for less. It's for:

- Workers aiming higher: Those who want to climb the ladder but don't know where to start.

- Entrepreneurs scaling fast: Those who are building businesses and need a proven framework to grow.

- Individuals redefining their path: Those who are ready to take control and build something extraordinary.

This book is for people who don't wait for permission, but take action and create their own opportunities.

Your Future Starts Now

My Sardinian roots taught me the value of hard work and resilience. But your future depends on what you do today. I've distilled a lifetime of lessons from my family, my mentors, and my own experiences into this book to give you a clear, actionable plan. Success is not about luck, it's about building, step by step, until you reach your goals.

The tools are here. The plan is clear. All that's left is for you to take the first step. Turn the page and start building something unstoppable.

PART ONE

The Foundations: Building the Personal Base

1

Early Foundations

"The foundations of a building are often hidden beneath the surface, but they are the most important part. Without them, the structure can't stand. Similarly, the early experiences and lessons in life are the hidden foundations that shape who we become." Mr. Ibba

My journey into the world of construction began before I even understood what a career could be. I was just a young child, barely four years old, when I started learning about the tools and processes that would shape the course of my life. For many, childhood is a time for play, but for me, it was the beginning of a deep relationship with the world of building one that would influence everything I did from that moment on. Growing up in a family of builders, I was immersed in a world where craftsmanship, discipline, and attention to detail were not just values they were the foundation of everything we did. My father was a builder, and my grandfather was an entrepreneur and a skilled saddle maker. From them, I learned the importance of precision, the value of hard work, and the unwavering commitment to excellence. These lessons, passed down through generations, shaped the way I approach both my work and life. In construction, every project begins with a solid base, and the same applies to personal and professional success. The principles of building discipline, resilience, and an eye for detail are the same principles that have guided me in my journey to build a successful business and mindset, one brick at a time.

The Hands-On Learning

From an early age, I was surrounded by workers who weren't just building they were creating, repairing, and restoring. Living in a small, old town in Sardinia, Italy, many of our projects involved the restoration of houses over 200 years old. These homes were built on foundations of stone, rising about a meter high, with walls made from bricks crafted from a mixture of mud and straw. The weight of history pressed down on each structure, and with every restoration, we had to carefully preserve what had withstood centuries. It was a challenging environment, especially given the constant dust and debris created during the restoration process. But that dust, as messy and relentless as it could be, carried with it the spirit of craftsmanship each project a journey through time, piecing together fragments of the past.

Whether it was fixing a leak, wiring an electrical system, or putting up a new wall, I was fascinated by the process. Every time a new project began, I'd be there, eager to understand how it all came together. Even though I was too young to contribute directly, I asked questions, endless questions. How did they know exactly where to place the walls? Why did certain materials go together while others didn't? I observed, absorbed, and learned. These early years were my real education in construction. In that environment, I quickly discovered that every task, no matter how small, had to be done with intention and precision. You couldn't cut corners and expect the result to stand the test of time.

In our town, the role of a builder wasn't just about laying bricks or plastering walls. The builder was everything; bricklayer, stonemason, electrician, plumber, carpenter, painter, and tiler. We wore many hats, and every project required a multifaceted approach. Restoration wasn't just about fixing physical structures; we had to solve problems which had often been hidden beneath layers of time. These were my first lessons in construction, and they were also my first lessons in life. The importance of building strong foundations wasn't just a concept I would later learn in business school; it was something I felt deep in my bones as I watched buildings take shape. Every nail hammered, every brick laid, was a lesson that would stay with me forever.

A Desire for More

With every task, I learned the principles of construction: measuring twice, cutting once; understanding how small details could impact the bigger picture; and appreciating the value of sweat equity. But it wasn't just physical labor. There was something about the way the builders talked, how they discussed the work, solved problems, and approached challenges that captivated me. These were men who were confident in their skills, who took pride in their craftsmanship. They didn't just build homes; they built with purpose, knowing that what they did would stand for decades to come. I wanted that confidence, that knowledge. I wanted to be someone who could not only understand the process but also control it. The more I learned, the more I wanted to be directly involved in shaping the work myself. But I knew it wasn't something that could be done overnight. This would be a journey, one that would take years, even decades, to fully understand.

Growing up, conversations at home were never about personal life or idle chatter. If we weren't on the building site with my father, we were working at the farm, harvesting grapes in autumn or handling some other task. Our discussions were always about the next job to do, the next step in the work. There was no room for anything else, no time for asking if I was planning to hang out with friends or enjoy any free time. Time to work was sacred, and the rest of life didn't really exist in those moments. As a teenager, that left me with a hunger for something more, a desire for deeper understanding and control over my own path. It wasn't enough to simply follow instructions or be part of the process. I wanted to know how to lead it, to be the one who called the shots, just as those builders did. And I knew that desire could only be fulfilled by dedicating myself fully to this journey, one that would require far more than just physical labor. It would require me to grow, learn, and push beyond the boundaries of what I thought was possible.

The Roots of Dedication and Passion

My early involvement in construction taught me something crucial: nothing worthwhile is easy. Every building project has its setbacks and mistakes. Similarly, life doesn't always go as planned. But the lesson I took from those years of watching others work was that if you wanted something to last, you had to be committed to putting in the effort, even when it seemed like the task was too big or the obstacles too great.

From a young age, I learned that there were no shortcuts. If a wall was crooked, it had to be fixed. If a mistake was made, it needed to be addressed before it could cause bigger problems down the line. This principle wasn't just about construction; it applied to every area of life. The lessons learned from these early experiences became my core values: commitment to quality, paying attention to the smallest of details, and not shying away from hard work.

By the time I reached my teenage years, I had already developed a deep love for construction and architecture. While most kids my age were focused on sports or hanging out with friends, I was spending my weekends building little devices with batteries, wires, and some other electric motors or helping out on job sites, learning as much as I could from those around me. At first, I was an assistant, carrying tools, sweeping the floors, or fetching materials. But slowly, I gained more responsibility.

Mastery in Every Detail: A Holistic Approach to Construction

From the beginning, I knew that to provide the best service, I needed to understand every facet of construction. It wasn't enough to specialize in just one area, like design or structural work; I wanted to be well-versed in everything; electrical, plumbing, gas, and more. This holistic approach stemmed from my belief that to deliver a truly exceptional product, you need to be an expert in every part of the building process.

As I grew older and gained more experience, this mindset became even more ingrained in my approach. If you want to build something that lasts, you can't afford to overlook the details, no matter how small they seem. I could have chosen to outsource certain parts of the process, trusting specialists in each field, but I always felt that having a deep understanding of each discipline gave me an edge.

By mastering the technical systems that go into every building, whether it's ensuring that electrical work is safe and up to code, the plumbing flows perfectly, or the gas systems are installed with precision,I could offer a complete, high-quality service to my clients. This approach not only ensured the buildings I worked on were structurally sound but also that every aspect of the project met the highest standards.This commitment to expertise became one of the cornerstones of my philosophy in both construction and business. Not only is it managing a team or overseeing a project, but also taking on any part of the process and making sure it's done right.

From Mistakes to Mastery: The Journey of Self-Learning

As I mentioned earlier, I wasn't one to listen to others or follow the established ways. Even though my father was a professional in the construction industry, I preferred to make my own mistakes. To me, failure was just a part of the learning process. Through trial and error, I developed true expertise across the entire building process.

All my mistakes, while frustrating, were invaluable teachers. Every misstep, whether it was choosing the wrong material or miscalculating a design element, taught me something new and made me better at what I did.

This self-reliance fostered a mindset of resilience and constant growth. I didn't shy away from challenges; instead, I embraced them because I knew that the mistakes I made today would only make me a stronger and more capable builder tomorrow. Looking back, I was proud, nearly arrogant in my ignorance. If I didn't know something, I tried anyway; I didn't care to ask for help. I was stubborn and unwilling to admit that I didn't have all the answers. I wanted to prove to myself, and perhaps to those around me, that I could figure it out on my own. But that pride was a double-edged sword. It led me into some frustrating situations, and it was a lesson I had to learn the hard way: that sometimes, asking for help or admitting you don't know something isn't a weakness, but a strength in itself.

The Power of Persistence: Resilience in the Face of Challenges

Just as in life, in construction, things don't always go according to plan. No matter how much preparation you put in, unexpected issues arise. What separates successful builders from the rest is the ability to stay persistent and resilient in the face of challenges.Throughout my career, I've faced countless obstacles. From design flaws to materials being delayed, misunderstanding the client, hiring the wrong person, or even unforeseen structural issues; there was no shortage of hurdles to overcome. But the difference between those who thrive and those who fail is how they handle setbacks.I've learned that no matter how difficult it may seem at the time, if you maintain your focus and keep pushing forward, you'll eventually find a way to solve the problem. It's about adapting quickly, staying calm under pressure, and always looking for solutions, not excuses. Resilience became my driving force, allowing me to face each day with a mindset focused on growth rather than defeat.Over the years, I've come to see resilience as one of the most important qualities a builder and a leader can have. When you understand that every setback is simply an opportunity to grow, you begin to shift your perspective and start viewing challenges as necessary stepping stones on the path to success.

Precision in Planning: A Step Forward to Success

A builder's mindset is incomplete without precision in planning. The success of every project lies in the planning process.

When I first started, I often underestimated how critical this step was. Early on, I was more focused on action, diving into projects without fully assessing every detail. Over time, I realized that careful planning is just as important as hard work.

Each project, no matter how big or small, deserves thorough planning. This involves strategically thinking through every possible outcome, considering contingencies for when things go wrong, and clearly defining the roles and responsibilities of everyone involved. The more detailed your plan, the easier it is to navigate challenges when they arise. Through this process, I learned that to truly excel in life, as a builder and a business owner, I needed to think like an architect. Not only do you have to design the structure, but you also need to design the process, how the work will unfold, how the team will communicate, and how each part of the project fits together. Planning became my tool for success. It allowed me to foresee potential obstacles, address them proactively, and move forward with confidence. It was through this discipline that I learned to avoid costly mistakes and make smarter decisions that saved both time and resources.

Attention to Detail: Craftsmanship in Every Aspect

Construction is more than just a job; it's an art form. Every beam, every nail, every corner of a building requires careful attention to detail. As I grew more experienced, I realized that the true value of a craftsman lies in their ability to perfect the smallest details. It's the subtle touches; the things that might not be immediately visible to the untrained eye that make the difference between an average job and one that stands out.My obsession with excellence was something I learned from my grandfather. He was an extraordinary saddle maker, crafting saddles and tack for horses and donkeys with an unmatched level of skill. I can still remember the rich scent of leather filling his workshop, mixed with the sharp, distinctive smell of pitch used to coat the sewing thread. It was a job he often assigned to me, soaking the threads in pitch to strengthen them while he focused on stitching.

My grandfather's approach to his craft was meticulous. Every stitch had to be identical to the last, forming perfect, straight lines across the leather. Every cut was measured with absolute precision. There was no room for waste. His job wasn't just assembling pieces of leather; he created something that would last, something that was not only functional but beautiful.

Watching him work, I understood that craftsmanship isn't just a skill, it's being proud of what you create. He never settled for "good enough" and neither did I. Whether it was a finely stitched saddle or a perfectly aligned window frame, I adopted the same relentless pursuit of perfection. This commitment to detail is something I instilled in my team as well. No matter how big or small the task, I encouraged them to approach each part of the job with the same level of dedication. When you treat every task with care and exactitude, it becomes part of a larger effort to build something truly remarkable. It's not just about finishing a project, it's about leaving behind a legacy of quality, one detail at a time.

Reflect on Your Foundations

Take a moment to reflect on how your own early experiences have shaped your life and career.

Think about an experience from your childhood that influenced your approach to work or life. How did it shape you? Write down your reflections and consider how these lessons can guide you today. For example, a simple task like helping around the house might have taught you discipline or responsibility values you can apply to your current goals.

For me, watching my father and grandfather work taught me the value of precision and hard work, lessons that continue to guide me. Try this exercise to uncover the foundations that shape your own path.

Conclusion: Laying the Groundwork for a Lasting Legacy

The lessons I learned in those early years in Sardinia were more than just the building blocks of my career they were the foundation of my life. They taught me that success, whether in construction or in life, begins with a strong base: a commitment to hard work, a dedication to precision, and the resilience to keep going, no matter the challenge. As I moved forward, these principles guided me through every project and every setback, setting the stage for the journey of rebuilding that would come later; a journey we'll explore in the next chapter.

"Sa Buttega De Su Sedderi" The Saddler's Workshop. This is where I learned to stay quiet and watch. Where I understood what real work means. This is where it all began.

"Su Maistu de muru" The Builder. This photo takes me back to my childhood, when I breathed the air of construction sites, surrounded by hardworking masons like these. It's where my journey in construction began.

*Pieces of Sardegna. My first 250-year-old house
renovation back in the 1987.*

2

The Role of Family and Tradition in Building Success

"Family is everything. It's the foundation of society, the institution people rely on for support, love, and strength. Just like wolves, who live in packs, we thrive within our families, drawing strength from one another to face the challenges of the world."
Mr Ibba

Introduction: The Cornerstones of Identity and Strength

Family and tradition are two pillars that shape our lives in ways both profound and enduring. They are the unseen forces that guide us, inform our values, and provide the foundation upon which we build our personal and professional identities. From childhood to adulthood, the lessons we learn within the family unit and the customs passed down through generations influence who we become, how we behave, and ultimately, how we interact with the world around us.

Growing up in a family with five sisters, I was the center of attention, especially because my parents wanted a son and didn't give up until I was born. That feeling of being wanted, of being the one they had hoped for, stayed with me throughout my life. I remember a time when our family was incredibly united, not just by love but by work and shared experiences. My father and my uncle built their houses next to my grandfather's, and the homes formed a circle around a common courtyard.

This space was the heart of our family life, where we did everything together: harvesting grapes for wine, preparing meat, and every family member contributed to creating something together.

The bonds were not only emotional but practical. We shared everything: food, work, and chores. If one person was missing, nothing stopped, because we trusted each other. Every family member was an artisan, so when one of us wasn't around, work and activities continued without interruption because we were all equally capable. We celebrated every occasion together: birthdays, weddings, and significant moments in life. The sense of unity was unbreakable.

But it wasn't just our family that lived like this; in our village, this sense of unity was common. Families supported each other; sharing work, traditions, and challenges. There was a sense of community that went beyond blood ties, where everyone took care of one another as if they were part of their own family. This spirit of collaboration and trust was an integral part of everyone's life. My grandparents lived with us until the end, and when they could no longer care for themselves, we took turns looking after them. It was a true community, a system of mutual support built on care and respect. This taught me the importance of family, unity, and working together to build something lasting.

In business, much like in life, these elements play a critical role in shaping our approach to leadership, decision-making, and resilience in the face of adversity. This chapter explores the role that family and tradition play in forming our character, enhancing our professional success, and fostering sustainable, long-term growth.

The Influence of Family: Building Character from the Start

Our earliest lessons come from those closest to us; our families. The values, behaviors, and attitudes that are instilled in us from childhood have a significant impact on our future endeavors, including the decisions we make in business. Family is where we first learn about responsibility, trust, respect, and loyalty. These foundational principles shape not only our personal identity but also our professional interactions.

The Role of Family in Shaping Success:

- Nurturing Accountability: Families provide the first environment where we are held accountable for our actions. Learning to take responsibility from a young age lays the groundwork for strong leadership. Accountability in the home environment mirrors the expectations we carry into business, where the ability to own both successes and failures is crucial for growth.

- Cultivating a Strong Work Ethic: Through direct experience and by observing parents and caregivers, the example set in a family can be an enduring motivator for professional achievement.

- Fostering Emotional Intelligence: Family life often requires empathy, understanding, and negotiation. These qualities, honed within the family unit, can directly translate into high emotional intelligence, which is a crucial trait for effective leadership and relationship-building in business.

The Intersection of Family and Tradition: Guiding Business Leadership

Leadership, whether in a home setting or in business, is deeply influenced by the intertwined dynamics of family and tradition. The way we lead at home often shapes how we lead at work. Similarly, the traditions that were fostered in our families guide the values and principles we apply in our business practices. This unique intersection of family and tradition can define how we manage our teams, make critical decisions, and lead by example.

Leading by Example:

- Modeling Behavior: In the family environment, parents and guardians model behavior that children internalize. The leadership demonstrated in the home often translates into leadership styles in the workplace. A leader who values honesty, integrity, and hard work is more likely to instill those same values in their business operations, creating a cohesive, aligned team.

- Resilience in the Face of Adversity: Family traditions often include navigating difficult times together, teaching resilience, persistence, and collaboration. In business, these same qualities are essential for overcoming challenges and leading a company through economic downturns, market shifts, or internal changes.

The Role of Family in Business Ownership: Balancing Legacy with Growth

For entrepreneurs who inherit or build family businesses, the relationship between family and business becomes even more complex. Balancing the legacy of family values with the drive for innovation and growth can be a delicate task, but it's one that can offer tremendous rewards when approached with the right mindset.

Challenges of Family-Owned Businesses:

- Generational Transition: One of the primary challenges facing family businesses is the transition of leadership between generations. Often, successors must navigate the expectations of maintaining family traditions while adapting to modern business needs.

- Cultural Continuity vs. Innovation: The challenge of maintaining tradition while embracing innovation is a balancing act that many family businesses face. Preserving the legacy and culture of the family business while ensuring it stays relevant and competitive in an ever-changing marketplace requires a delicate blend of honoring tradition and embracing new ideas.

Strategies for Success:

- Formalizing Processes: One of the most effective ways to ensure the success of a family business is by creating clear structures and processes that allow for both tradition and innovation. This might include codifying values within the company's mission and vision statements while also encouraging flexibility in operational practices.

- Succession Planning: Preparing the next generation for leadership in a family business is crucial. This involves not just passing down the business but also passing down the skills, values, and traditions that make it unique.

Family, Tradition, and Resilience: Thriving Through Adversity

Adversity is an inevitable part of life and business, but it's often through challenging times that the influence of family and tradition becomes most evident. Both family values and traditions serve as sources of strength, resilience, and support in navigating difficult situations.

Building Resilience Through Family Support:

- Learning from Adversity: Family traditions often include overcoming challenges together, teaching us how to face adversity with a positive mindset. These lessons of resilience become invaluable in the business world, where obstacles are part of the journey.

- Emotional Resilience: During times of hardship, families often provide emotional support. This helps individuals remain focused and motivated, even when external circumstances are challenging.

- Practical Guidance: Family members often provide valuable practical advice, especially if they have experience in business or other relevant fields. A family business, in particular, benefits from this kind of mentorship, where seasoned leaders guide younger generations through the complexities of running a company.

- Financial Support: While not all families can offer financial support, some family businesses rely on generational wealth and resources to get through tough financial times. This stability allows the business to grow and innovate without the constant worry of financial insecurity.

Tradition: Preserving Heritage, Building Legacy and Creating Lasting Impact

Tradition is more than just cultural or familial practices; it's a way of preserving the wisdom and values of those who came before us. Traditions are the threads that connect generations, weaving a continuous story that strengthens the sense of identity and purpose. This family culture helps maintain a sense of continuity through annual gatherings, cultural celebrations, and specific business practices.

At the heart of both family and business lies a desire to create something that lasts. Whether it's a business legacy or the continuation of familial traditions, the goal is often to create something enduring, something that will be passed down to future generations.

The Power of Tradition in Business:

- Creating Consistency: In business, tradition provides consistency. Companies that understand their roots and honor the traditions established by their founders often experience long-term success because they remain anchored to the values that helped them grow. For instance, businesses that prioritize customer relationships, quality craftsmanship, or ethical behavior are often those that continue to thrive through changing times.

- Enhancing Brand Identity: Just as families pass down cultural customs, businesses also build their own traditions and legacies. A strong brand identity is often tied to the traditions a company upholds, which influences its culture, customer relationships, and overall market reputation.

- Fostering Trust: Business traditions help build trust among employees, clients, and customers. When a company has a clear set of traditions and values, it cultivates loyalty both internally with its workforce and externally with its customer base.

Creating a Lasting Impact:

- Building for the Future: Both family values and business traditions contribute to the building of a legacy that transcends individual efforts. When family values and traditions are deeply embedded in a business, the legacy created isn't just about profitability, but also the impact made on the community, employees, and future generations.

- Leadership Beyond Generations: A strong family and business legacy provides the foundation for leadership that will guide future generations. By instilling the right values in both personal and professional lives, individuals create an enduring impact that continues to inspire.

The Role of Family in Decision-Making: A Crucial Influence

One of the most critical aspects of leadership and business management is decision-making. The values learned from family shape how individuals approach complex decisions. In business, these decisions can determine the future of a company, its profitability, and its reputation. The lessons from family life often influence the choices made in the professional sphere.

How Family Influences Decision-Making:

- Learning to Weigh Priorities: Family life teaches us to balance multiple priorities. At home, individuals learn to juggle relationships, responsibilities, and goals, which directly translate into how they approach business decisions. Business leaders who prioritize their family values often weigh their decisions with a holistic view, considering the impact on both their business and personal lives.

- Developing Ethical Decision-Making: The principles of fairness, honesty, and integrity learned within the family unit often guide business leaders in making ethical decisions. These values are crucial when faced with difficult choices, as they ensure that decisions are made in the best interest of all stakeholders, from employees to customers.

- Considering Long-Term Impact: Family-based decision-making often involves long-term thinking. For example, parents make decisions that affect their children's futures. Similarly, business leaders who value their family's legacy tend to make decisions that will benefit the company for years to come, rather than opting for short-term gains.

Family as the Foundation for Entrepreneurial Spirit

Entrepreneurship requires more than just a good idea it requires a mindset that is shaped by experiences, values, and lessons learned from early influences. For many successful entrepreneurs, the seeds of their entrepreneurial spirit were planted within their families.

How Family Fosters Entrepreneurial Traits:

- Risk-Taking and Innovation: Family environments that encourage creativity and problem-solving foster an entrepreneurial mindset. Children raised in households where risks are embraced, whether in starting new ventures or trying unconventional solutions, often develop a natural inclination toward entrepreneurship.

- Self-Reliance and Independence: Many family units teach the value of self-reliance, which directly correlates with the entrepreneurial spirit. From managing personal chores to taking on leadership roles in family projects, individuals who grow up with a sense of independence are more likely to venture into entrepreneurship and pursue innovative ideas.

- Resilience to Failure: The family environment also teaches resilience to failure. Just as parents encourage children to try again after a failure, successful entrepreneurs often view setbacks as learning experiences rather than as barriers to success. This mindset is critical in navigating the inevitable challenges that come with running a business.

Tradition as a Guiding Principle for Leadership and Governance

In the business world, leadership and governance are crucial for sustainable success. Many business leaders look to the traditions within their families for guidance on how to lead with integrity and responsibility. Tradition is not just about preserving practices but embedding principles that guide leadership and influence company culture.

Leadership Through Tradition:

- Preserving Core Values: Many successful leaders come from families that emphasize core values, such as integrity, humility, and accountability. These values become ingrained in how they lead and influence the company culture. Business leaders who uphold these traditions often inspire loyalty and trust among their teams.

- Stewardship of Legacy: Business leaders who come from family backgrounds with a strong sense of tradition often feel a responsibility to protect and grow the family's legacy. This stewardship can shape decisions related to business expansion, acquisitions, and partnerships.

- Fostering a Culture of Respect: Traditions within families often emphasize the importance of respect for elders, peers or others. In business, leaders who value respect create a culture of inclusivity and empowerment, where employees feel valued and appreciated. This kind of leadership promotes a positive and productive work environment.

The Role of Family and Tradition in Social Responsibility

Successful business leaders understand the importance of giving back to their communities, and often, the motivation for this sense of social responsibility comes from family values and traditions. Many family businesses are built on the idea that success is not just about personal gain, but also about contributing to the broader good.

Corporate Social Responsibility:

- Ethical Responsibility: Families that prioritize ethical behavior and giving often pass these values down to future generations. In business, this translates into a commitment to corporate social responsibility (CSR).

Family-owned businesses are often at the forefront of charitable giving, environmental responsibility, and ethical sourcing.

- Building Community Relationships: Traditions of community involvement, for example through volunteering, mentorship, or philanthropy, are often passed from one generation to the next. These traditions help businesses build meaningful relationships with their communities, leading to long-term loyalty and trust.

- Sustainability Practices: Many businesses that honor family traditions also value sustainability, passing down practices that promote environmental stewardship and sustainability. This commitment to the planet's future is often seen as a continuation of the family's legacy and responsibility.

The Multigenerational Impact of Family-Owned Businesses

Family-owned businesses have a unique ability to thrive across multiple generations. This longevity is often a result of family members working together to build on the foundation set by previous generations. The values, traditions, and knowledge passed down through the family create a strong sense of continuity and purpose. Each generation contributes its own perspectives while honoring the legacy that came before it.

These businesses are built on trust, shared vision, and a deep understanding of the family's goals, which fosters a strong commitment to success and long-term sustainability.

The way family members work together strengthens the bond, allowing for innovation and adaptation while staying true to core values. The lessons learned from overcoming challenges, whether in the business or personal lives, are shared and contribute to resilience. This multi-generational approach allows for a business that is not only financially prosperous but also culturally rich, with a deep sense of identity rooted in the family's history and vision. The continuity of purpose across generations gives family-owned businesses an edge in building trust with customers, employees, and communities. Ultimately, these businesses transcend mere commerce, creating a lasting impact on the family, the business itself, and society as a whole.

Much like the Rockefeller family, which has successfully maintained a business legacy built on strong values and vision, family-owned businesses can become pillars of strength, innovation, and resilience across generations. Their ability to evolve while staying grounded in their foundational principles has allowed them to not only survive but thrive. In contrast, the Vanderbilts are an example of a family that squandered the wealth and business legacy built by their patriarch, Cornelius Vanderbilt. Despite the enormous fortune he amassed through railroads and shipping, successive generations failed to maintain the same discipline, focus, and unity. As a result, much of the family's wealth was dissipated, showing how neglecting core values and failing to collaborate as a unified family can lead to the collapse of a legacy. The story of the Vanderbilts serves as a stark reminder of the importance of responsibility, foresight, and cooperation in preserving a family business across generations.

Conclusion: The Enduring Power of Family and Tradition

Family and tradition are not just a part of my life they are the very essence of who I am and the cornerstone of everything I've built. The values of unity, resilience, and craftsmanship I learned in Sardinia gave me the strength to face every challenge, from personal setbacks to the trials of starting a business. When I took my first steps into entrepreneurship, these lessons became my guiding light, steering me through the chaos of building a company from the ground up a journey we'll explore in the next chapter.

But family and tradition are not relics of the past; they are a living, breathing force that continues to shape my present and future. Every decision I make, every project I undertake, is infused with the values rooted in the courtyard of my childhood home, where it all began. And as I look ahead, I know that this foundation will not only support me but also those who come after me. Because, in the end, true success is not just about what we build, but what we leave behind.

Take a moment to reflect on your roots. What values have you inherited from your family? How can they guide you today, in this moment? Remember: the foundations we lay today will determine how high we can rise tomorrow.

3

Business Beginnings: A Wake-Up Call

"The secret of getting ahead is getting started." Mark Twain

I was a teenager when I started my first business. It was no overnight success, and the journey was filled with challenges. But those struggles gave me the epiphanies I needed to grow me as a leader and a human being. These countless lessons laid the groundwork for a sustainable business.

The First Major Setback: A Lesson in Reality

At the age of 16, I made a decision that would change the course of my life: I decided I didn't want to work for my father anymore. I thought I knew everything there was to know about construction after all; I had spent years watching, learning, and working by his side. I believed I could do it on my own, that I could be my own boss, call the shots, and reap the rewards. I had no idea what I was getting myself into. I thought being a business owner meant freedom and success, but I quickly learned that it's about responsibility, and that meant owning every decision, every mistake, and every outcome. There was no safety net, no one to fall back on when things went wrong. It was all on me, and that realization hit me like a freight train.

The transition from being an employee to owning my own construction business was nothing short of a wake-up call. I thought I had a solid understanding of how things worked. I knew how to build, how to use tools, how to design, but the reality of running a business was far more complex. It wasn't just about technical skills; it was about managing every moving part of a business. I wasn't prepared for the long hours, the stress, and the constant decision-making. I was so caught up in my own pride, so convinced that my limited experience was enough, that I didn't grasp the true weight of what I had taken on.

My father had spent 50 years learning how to build and run a business in this industry. Yet here I was, thinking that after just a couple of years mostly spent sweeping floors and unloading trucks of sand, brick, or cement, I knew it all. The confidence I had in my abilities was naïve, and it became painfully clear that there was so much more to starting a business than laying bricks or installing pipes. I had underestimated the depth of knowledge, adaptability, and humility required to succeed as an entrepreneur. That realization was humbling, but it was also the spark that ignited my journey.

In the early days of my business, I was eager to prove myself. I secured my first major contract, a small residential project to renovate a 100-year-old house in a rural Sardinian village. The client, a local family, had high expectations, and I saw this as my chance to establish a reputation for quality and reliability. I threw myself into the project with all the energy I had, confident that my skills would carry me through. But I made a critical mistake: I overestimated my abilities and underestimated the project's complexity. The house was built with traditional ladiri mud and straw bricks that were fragile and required specialized techniques to handle. I had worked with these materials before, but I didn't account for the structural challenges of the site. The foundation was uneven, and the walls were more deteriorated than I had anticipated. Instead of seeking advice from a more experienced builder or conducting a thorough assessment, I pushed forward, relying on my instincts.

Halfway through the project, disaster struck. During a stormy week, one of the walls we had begun to restore collapsed overnight. The sound of the crash woke the neighbors, and by morning, the client was at the site, furious and worried about the safety of the entire structure. I stood there, staring at the rubble, feeling the weight of my failure. I had let down the client, endangered the project, and risked my reputation, all because I had been too proud to admit I needed help. That moment was my epiphany. I couldn't run a business on what I already knew, but instead I would only succeed by acknowledging what I had yet to learn. I had to find a way to skill up, adapt and grow. I had to salvage the project, rebuild the client's trust, and ensure this failure became a stepping stone rather than a breaking point. I spent the next few days working tirelessly to fix the damage. I hired an experienced engineer to assess the foundation, sourced the right materials to reinforce the structure, and worked closely with the client to revise the timeline. By the time the project was complete, the house was stronger than ever, and the client's trust in me was restored not because I had avoided failure, but because I had faced it head on.

The Hidden Challenges of Starting a Business

The construction industry is not for the faint-hearted. The competition is fierce, the stakes are high, and the margin for error is slim. Every project presents unexpected hurdles, whether it's a sudden storm, a delayed shipment of materials, or a client's last-minute request for changes. In those early days, I quickly realized that starting a business required a level of adaptability I hadn't anticipated. I couldn't afford to get stuck in my ways; I had to remain flexible and constantly assess how I could solve problems more efficiently.There were days when I found myself juggling multiple roles: managing budgets, overseeing workers on-site, and handling paperwork late into the night. Every task felt urgent, and everything seemed to need my attention immediately. But the hardest part was learning to manage my own expectations and emotions. I had to balance being assertive when necessary, ensuring timelines were met and standards were upheld, while also maintaining good relationships to foster collaboration. It was a fine line, and I often stumbled as I learned how to walk it.

Statistics paint a stark picture of the challenges new business owners face. According to studies, about 20% of small businesses fail within their first year, and nearly 50% don't survive past the fifth year. The reasons are often the same: lack of preparation, inability to adapt, and failure to seek help. These numbers aren't meant to discourage you. They're a reminder that starting a business requires more than just passion. It demands a mindset that sees setbacks as opportunities to learn and grow.

Overcoming Personal Challenges

While building my business, I also faced a slew of personal challenges. Juggling the demands of work with family life, relationship struggles, and emotional growth was tough. As a young father, I didn't always have the balance I needed. There were times when I would put work above everything else, thinking that financial success would make everything else fall into place. But the reality was far more complicated.

My emotional growth was just as important as my business growth. I learned that I couldn't be a great leader or business owner if I wasn't also taking care of myself mentally, emotionally, and physically. Over time, I realized that personal growth and business growth were interconnected. The more I worked on improving myself, the more I could give to my business, my clients, and my team. In the beginning, I had to push through my own insecurities, doubts, and fears. But as time went on, I developed more confidence and resilience. I started to believe in my abilities, trust my instincts, and let go of the need for perfection.

Navigating my personal relationships was no easier. I learned that business stress could bleed into my personal life, especially when things were tough. There were times when I felt emotionally drained and disconnected, which only made things harder. But eventually, I came to understand that growth, both personal and professional, isn't linear. There were peaks, valleys, and moments where it felt like nothing was going right. But I came out of each challenge stronger, more focused, and more determined to continue building.

The Cycle of Starting a Business: Vision, Risk, Adaptation

That first failed project taught me lessons I've carried with me throughout my entrepreneurial journey. From that experience, I developed a simple framework that I call the Cycle of Starting a Business. This cycle isn't about managing teams or scaling a company; those lessons will come later in this book. These are the foundational steps every entrepreneur must take to turn a dream into a reality, especially in those early, uncertain days.

Vision – Define Your Purpose: Before you start, you need a clear vision of what you want to achieve. For me, my vision was to build a construction company that delivered quality and reliability, rooted in the values I learned from my family. Your vision doesn't have to be grand,avoid, it just has to be yours. What do you want your business to stand for? Take the time to define your purpose, because it will guide every decision you make.

Risk – Embrace the Unknown: Starting a business is inherently risky. You'll face challenges you can't predict, like I did with that crumbling wall. But risk isn't something to avoid, it's something to embrace. The key is to take calculated risks: understand what you're getting into, prepare as much as you can, and be ready to adapt when things go wrong. Risk is the price of entry for any new venture, and the sooner you accept it, the better equipped you'll be to handle it.

Adaptation – Learn and Pivot: The difference between failure and success often lies in your ability to adapt. When that wall collapsed, I could have let it define my business. Instead, I learned from my mistake, adjusted my approach, and turned a failure into a foundation. Adaptation means being willing to change, to seek help, and to grow through every challenge. It's not about being perfect, it's about being resilient in the face of the unexpected.

This cycle, Vision, Risk, Adaptation, is a roadmap for navigating the early days of a business. It's a reminder that starting a business is a journey of growth, not a race to perfection. Every entrepreneur will face setbacks, but those who can adapt and learn from their mistakes are the ones who build something lasting.

Turning Your Beginnings into a Foundation for Success

If you're starting a business or even embarking on a new venture in your life, you'll face moments like the one I experienced with that collapsed wall. You'll make mistakes, you'll encounter setbacks, and you'll question whether you're cut out for the journey. But those moments are not the end they're the beginning of your growth. Here's how you can turn your business beginnings into a foundation for success:

Embrace Humility: Don't be afraid to admit what you don't know. Seek advice, ask questions, and surround yourself with people who can help you grow. I learned this the hard way when I had to hire an engineer to fix my mistake—humility saved my project and my reputation.

Prepare Thoroughly: Before you start, take the time to understand the challenges you'll face. Research your market, assess your resources, and plan for the unexpected. Preparation doesn't guarantee success, but it gives you the tools to navigate the unknown.

Learn from Failure: When things go wrong, don't give up. Analyze what happened, adjust your approach, and use the experience to build a stronger foundation. That failed project taught me more about running a business than any success ever could.

Think about a professional or entrepreneurial challenge you've faced in the past. What lesson did you learn from that experience? How can you apply it today to improve your approach? Write down three concrete actions you can take to turn that lesson into positive change. For example, if you learned the importance of clear communication, you might plan weekly meetings with your team to ensure everyone is aligned.

Conclusion: The Wake-Up Call That Built a Foundation

Looking back, that first failed project was more than just a wake-up call. It was the moment that shaped my entrepreneurial journey. It taught me that starting a business isn't about avoiding mistakes; it's about learning from them. It's about defining your vision, embracing the risks, and adapting to the challenges that come your way. Every entrepreneur's journey begins with a first step, and often, that step is a stumble. But if you're willing to learn, to adapt, and to keep going, that stumble can become the foundation of something extraordinary. The early days of my business were filled with hard lessons, but they set the stage for the life lessons I would learn through every project.

4

Rebuilding from the Ground Up: A Home to Bring My Daughter Back

"The brick walls are there for a reason. They are not there to keep us out. They are there to give us a chance to show how badly we want something." Randy Pausch

At the age of 19, I became a father, and at the time, I thought I had everything figured out. I had a family to provide for, and I was determined to give them the best life possible. But life has a way of throwing curveballs when you least expect it. After 10 years, my marriage ended, and I found myself starting over with nothing.

When the divorce happened, I didn't take anything from the house. I left everything behind with just the clothes on my back. I didn't care about the material things. What mattered to me in that moment was my family and my baby, not money or possessions. The decision to walk away from everything was one of the hardest choices I've ever made, but I did it for the right reasons.

I went back to my father's house, and it was a humbling experience. My ego took a huge hit. I had always prided myself on being independent, but here I was with nothing, back at home. It was hard to swallow. I remember that afternoon like it was yesterday; I went out to buy clothes because I didn't have any left.

After everything collapsed, I made a commitment to rebuild—not just my life, but a future that had meaning and purpose. This wasn't starting over; it was time to create something lasting, something that would allow me to provide for my daughter and offer her a stable home where she could feel safe and loved.

My Home, My Future

Building a house became my driving force. Every brick I laid and every wall I constructed symbolized more than just a structure; it was a foundation for a future I was determined to create. This construction was a testament to resilience, to the unwavering belief that I could build not just a home, but a new life.

The process of constructing my own home was, in many ways, an act of self-reclamation. It reminded me of my roots, my passion for building, and my ability to create something from nothing. Building that home wasn't easy. Each day brought new obstacles, but with every one, I grew stronger. The work itself became therapeutic. It was my way of proving to myself that no matter how far I had fallen, I had the strength to rise again. This was my second chance, and I refused to waste it.

And ultimately, it was all worth it. That house became the basis of my new life, a space where I could rebuild my world and welcome my daughter back into it.

The Importance of Never Giving Up

Success doesn't come easily. It requires persistence, grit, and the willingness to face adversity head-on. Each setback felt like a test. Could I keep going, even when everything seemed to be against me? The answer was always yes. I refused to quit, pushing forward day after day, even when the weight of past failures felt overwhelming. The more I focused on the process, the less I worried about the outcome, and in doing so, I made progress, one day at a time.

Through this experience, I discovered a profound truth: we are never as far down as we think we are. No matter how bad things seem, there is always a way to rise again. The key is to keep our focus on the bigger picture and never lose sight of the goals we set for ourselves.

The mindset that carried me through this period is one I live by to this day: no matter what happens, never give up. Success takes time, setbacks will come, but with persistence, anything is possible.

Turning Pain Into Purpose: Building a Legacy Beyond Ourselves

The struggles I endured weren't just about surviving hardship, they were about transformation. I took the pain of loss, failure, and uncertainty and forged them into something meaningful–something that could extend beyond my own life.

The pain of losing Sofia drove me to rebuild my life in a way I never would have otherwise. It gave me a purpose that went beyond myself, a reason to keep going when everything felt hopeless.

At first, my battle felt deeply personal. I was fighting to rebuild after setbacks that could have broken me. But as I worked, my perspective shifted. I realized that what I was building wasn't just about me I was creating a legacy. I would use my experiences to pave the way for others.

The house I built wasn't just walls and a roof; it was a declaration of resilience, perseverance, and the unshakable belief that no matter how many times life knocks us down, we can rise again. It was a testament to the transformative power of pain. And more importantly, it was a lesson for my daughter and for those who would come after me.

I thought deeply about the values I wanted to instill: the power of hard work, the necessity of resilience, and the truth that struggle is not an end but the beginning of something greater. I wanted my daughter to see that success isn't given; it is built, brick by brick, decision by decision, sacrifice by sacrifice.

I came to understand that true fulfillment doesn't come from personal success alone, but comes from what we build for others; my daughter, my family, my team. The most influential people in history weren't those who lived solely for themselves, but those who transformed their pain into a force for change.

The Transformative Power of Pain: A Universal Truth

Pain is universal. Whether it comes from a personal loss, a professional setback, or a shattered dream, it has the power to push us toward transformation. I've seen it in the lives of countless builders, entrepreneurs, and friends over the years. A contractor I met years ago lost his business in a recession, but the pain of that failure drove him to start anew, eventually building a company twice as successful as the first. A mother I knew lost her husband to illness, but through her grief, she founded a charity that has helped hundreds of families. Pain, when channeled into purpose, can become the foundation for something greater than you ever imagined. At some point, everyone faces hardship, heartbreak, or failure. But pain is also a tool—it can destroy us, or it can build us. If we allow it, adversity can become the very thing that fuels our purpose.

True greatness is not measured by what we accumulate, but by what we contribute. It is not defined by personal triumph, but by the number of lives we touch because we dared to turn our suffering into service.

The Science of Transformation: How Pain Fuels Growth

The idea that pain can lead to growth isn't just anecdotal, it's backed by science. Psychologists call this phenomenon post-traumatic growth, a process where individuals who experience significant adversity emerge stronger, more resilient, and with a renewed sense of purpose. Research shows that people who channel their pain into meaningful action often experience profound personal growth. They report greater appreciation for life, stronger relationships, and a clearer sense of what truly matters.

For me, building that house for Sofia was more than just a physical act, it was a psychological transformation. The pain of losing her gave me a clarity I hadn't had before, a focus on what truly mattered. It taught me to prioritize love over pride, connection over achievement, and purpose over perfection. And in the process, I became a better father, a better builder, and a better man.

The Pain-to-Purpose Framework: Turning Loss into Gain

Through my experience, I developed a simple framework to help me and others transform pain into purpose: the Pain-to-Purpose Framework. This framework isn't about resilience or persistence; it's about using your deepest pain as a catalyst to rebuild your life with intention and meaning.

Feel – Honor Your Pain: The first step is to feel your pain fully, without trying to suppress it. Don't run from it, don't numb it. Let it be. For me, this meant allowing myself to grieve the loss of my marriage and the distance from Sofia. I had to sit with the emptiness, to cry the tears I had held back, to acknowledge how much it hurt. Honoring your pain isn't a sign of weakness; it's a necessary step toward healing and growth.

Focus – Find Your Why: Once you've felt the pain, focus on finding a purpose, a "why" that gives your pain meaning. For me, my why was Sofia. I wanted to build a home where she could return to me, a place where we could rebuild our bond. Your why doesn't have to be a person; it could be a dream, a cause, or a vision for your future. Ask yourself: What can this pain inspire me to create?

Forge – Build with Intention: The final step is to channel your pain into action, building something new with intention. For me, this meant pouring my grief into the construction of that house, every nail a step toward bringing Sofia back. Whatever your pain, use it to fuel your efforts as you rebuild. Whether you're starting a new project, pursuing a dream, or healing a relationship, let your pain be the fire that drives you to forge something meaningful.

This framework helped me turn the darkest moment of my life into one of my greatest achievements. It's a process that anyone can use to transform their pain into a purpose that rebuilds their life.

The Pain-to-Purpose Framework isn't limited to construction or parenting, it can be applied to any area of life. Imagine an entrepreneur who loses a major client: they can Feel the disappointment, Focus on finding new opportunities, and Forge a strategy to rebuild their business. Or consider a student who fails an important exam: they can Feel the frustration, Focus on mastering the material, and Forge a study plan to excel in the next test. Whatever your struggle, this framework can help you turn pain into a catalyst for growth.

Pain-to-Purpose Reflection

Take a moment to reflect on a painful experience in your own life. How can you apply the Pain-to-Purpose Framework to turn that pain into something meaningful?

Feel (2 minutes): Write down the emotions you felt during that experience. Don't hold back. Let yourself fully acknowledge the pain.

Focus (2 minutes): Identify one meaningful purpose that could emerge from this pain. What can you create or achieve as a result?

Forge (1 minute): Choose one actionable step you can take this week to start building toward that purpose. Commit to it with intention.

For me, this exercise helped me see my pain as a starting point for something greater. Try it for yourself. It's a powerful way to transform adversity into action.

Conclusion: Building a Legacy from Your Pain

Building a home for Sofia wasn't just about providing a physical space, it was about rebuilding my life and my daughter's future from the ground up. Now, every house I build, every business I grow, and every lesson I share is part of something greater than myself. I aim to empower those who come after me, creating a roadmap for those who feel lost or broken, and proving that no matter where you come from or what you've endured, you can build something extraordinary, not just for yourself, but for the world.

We all have that power. We all have the ability to turn pain into purpose, to take what tried to break us and use it to build something unbreakable.

As I continued my journey, I carried this lesson with me, applying it not just to my personal life but to the ingenuity I would need to rebuild my business; a story we'll explore in the next chapter.

5

A Million Reasons to Make Sacrifices

"Success isn't a gift bestowed upon us; it's a garden cultivated through the sacrifices we choose to make." Mr. Ibba

Throughout my journey as a builder and entrepreneur, I've learned that nothing worth having comes without sacrifice. The houses we build, the businesses we grow, the lives we create, they all require us to give up something in the present to gain something greater in the future. Sacrifice isn't about loss; it's about investment. It's about choosing to plant seeds today so you can harvest a bountiful tomorrow. This chapter isn't about the hard work required to succeed, the resilience to overcome setbacks, or the relationships that support your journey. Those lessons are explored elsewhere in this book. It's about understanding sacrifice as a strategic choice, a deliberate decision to prioritize long-term gains over short-term comforts, and the profound rewards that come from that choice.

In my life, I've made countless sacrifices, but one moment stands out as a defining example of how sacrifice can lead to a legacy that lasts. It was a choice that tested my resolve, reshaped my priorities, and ultimately brought me closer to the life I wanted for myself and for my daughter.

The Sacrifice That Changed Everything

In the mid-2000s, my construction business faced a critical juncture. I had established a strong reputation for quality work, but I was primarily handling smaller projects, such as residential homes and renovations. My ambition was to scale the company and take on larger commercial endeavors that could leave a significant mark on the community. An opportunity arose to bid on a substantial contract for a public building project in a nearby area the largest I had ever pursued. Securing it would represent a major leap forward for my business, but it came with challenges: the timeline was tight, and the budget demanded a significant upfront investment of nearly all my company's resources.

At the same time, I had committed to taking a break, a rare chance to step away from my demanding schedule. This pause was something I hadn't done in years, and I valued the opportunity to recharge. However, accepting the project meant abandoning that plan and dedicating all my time, energy, and finances to the job. It was a tough call: short-term relief versus a long-term gain that could transform my business.

I deliberated for days, weighing the immediate comfort against the potential for growth. Ultimately, I chose to pursue the project, recognizing its importance not just for my own goals but for the future stability of the business. I explained my decision to those affected, promising to make up for the missed opportunity later if the project succeeded. Their understanding fueled my resolve.

I threw everything into that project long hours, financial reserves, and relentless focus, often staying on-site to ensure every detail was perfect. The effort was exhausting, but it paid off. The project was completed on schedule, and its quality elevated my reputation, opening doors to bigger contracts. The financial stability that followed allowed me to take a well-earned break the next year, one that surpassed what I had originally planned. That choice wasn't just about a single job; it was about building a foundation for sustained success, proving that strategic sacrifices can yield rewards far beyond the initial cost.

Sacrifice as a Strategic Choice

Sacrifice isn't about giving up for the sake of suffering, it's about making a strategic choice to prioritize long-term gains over short-term comforts. In construction, we often have to sacrifice time, resources, or immediate profit to ensure a building's longevity. We choose the stronger foundation over the cheaper one, even if it costs more upfront, because we know it will stand the test of time. In life, the same principle applies. Sacrifice means choosing the path that aligns with your ultimate goals, even if it means giving up something you value in the moment.

I've seen this play out in the lives of countless builders, entrepreneurs, and parents over the years. A contractor I knew sacrificed weekends with his family to attend trade school, eventually becoming a master craftsman whose work is renowned across Sardinia. A single mother I met gave up her social life to work two jobs, ensuring her children could attend university. These sacrifices weren't easy, but they were deliberate choices; investments in a future that was worth more than the immediate cost.

The rewards of sacrifice are profound. When I chose to take on that school project, I gained more than a contract. I gained financial stability, a stronger reputation, and the ability to give my daughter experiences I never could have afforded otherwise. Sacrifice isn't about loss; it's about gain. It's about understanding that every choice you make shapes the structure of your life, and sometimes, the greatest structures require the greatest investments.

Why Sacrifice Makes Sense: The Lasting Rewards

Sacrifice might feel daunting in the moment, but it makes sense when you consider the lasting rewards it brings. Over the years, I've come to see sacrifice not as a burden, but as a gateway to outcomes that make the cost worthwhile. Here are a million reasons distilled into a few key truths why sacrifice is a choice worth making:

It Builds a Stronger Future: Sacrifices create the foundation for a future that's more stable and secure than the present. By giving up that vacation with my daughter, I was able to build a business that provided for her education, her dreams, and our shared experiences. Sacrifice ensures that the future you're building is stronger than the moment you're letting go.

It Deepens Your Commitment: When you sacrifice something for a goal, you become more invested in its outcome. Canceling that vacation wasn't just about time, it was a signal to myself that I was all in on the school project, that I was committed to making it a success. Sacrifice turns your goals from wishes into imperatives, driving you to see them through.

It Teaches You What Truly Matters: Sacrifice forces you to clarify your priorities, revealing what you value most. Choosing the school project over the vacation showed me that my deepest priority was Sofia's long-term well-being, not just a fleeting moment of joy. Sacrifice strips away the superficial and brings clarity to what's truly important in your life.

It Creates Exponential Growth: The rewards of sacrifice often grow exponentially over time. The financial stability from that school project didn't just pay for one vacation, it funded years of opportunities for Sofia, from extracurricular activities to travel. Sacrifice plants seeds that grow into harvests far greater than the initial cost.

It Inspires Others: Your sacrifices don't just benefit you, they set an example for those around you. Seeing my commitment to the school project inspired Sofia to value hard work and dedication in her own life, shaping her into the driven young woman she is today. Sacrifice shows others what's possible when you choose the long-term over the immediate.

These reasons remind us that sacrifice isn't a loss, it's an investment in a future that's worth far more than what you give up. It's a choice that builds, grows, and inspires, creating a legacy that lasts beyond the moment.

The Sacrifice Evaluation Framework: Choosing What to Give Up

Making sacrifices isn't about giving up everything, it's about choosing the right sacrifices, the ones that align with your ultimate goals. Over the years, I've developed a simple framework to help me evaluate and make sacrifices strategically: the Sacrifice Evaluation Framework. This framework isn't about enduring hardships or pushing through challenges; it's about making deliberate choices that lead to long-term rewards.

Clarify Your Goal – Define What Matters Most: Start by identifying your ultimate goal the thing that matters most to you. For me, this was building a stable future for Sofia, which the school project would help me achieve. In your life, it might be starting a business, pursuing a passion, or providing for your family. Ask yourself: What am I building toward?

Weigh the Cost – Assess the Sacrifice: Next, evaluate what you'll need to give up to achieve that goal. Be honest about the cost both in the short term and the long term. For me, this meant giving up the family vacation and months of time with Sofia. In your life, it might mean giving up leisure time, financial security, or a comfortable routine. Ask yourself: What am I willing to sacrifice, and is the cost worth the reward?

Commit with Intention – Make the Choice: Finally, commit to the sacrifice with intention, knowing that it's a step toward your goal. For me, this meant explaining my decision to Sofia and promising to make it up to her later. In your life, it might mean setting boundaries, communicating your choice to loved ones, or mentally preparing for the challenge. The goal is to make the sacrifice a deliberate act, not a passive loss.

This framework: Clarify Your Goal, Weigh the Cost, Commit with Intention, helped me make the sacrifice for the school project, and it's a process I've used countless times since. It's a way to ensure that your sacrifices are strategic, aligned with your goals, and ultimately worth the cost.

The Science of Sacrifice: Why It Pays Off

Sacrifice might seem like a purely emotional choice, but it's also backed by science. Psychologists have found that delayed gratification, the ability to give up short-term rewards for long-term gains, is a key predictor of success. The famous Marshmallow Experiment showed that children who could resist eating a marshmallow to get a bigger reward later were more likely to achieve higher academic and professional success as adults. This principle, known as delayed gratification, applies to sacrifice as well. When I gave up that vacation with Sofia to take on the school project, I was practicing delayed gratification, choosing a future reward over immediate pleasure.

Neuroscience also shows that making sacrifices can rewire our brains for better decision-making. When we commit to a sacrifice, we activate the brain's prefrontal cortex, which is responsible for long-term planning and self-control. Over time, this strengthens our ability to make strategic choices, leading to greater success. For me, sacrificing the vacation wasn't just a one-time decision it trained me to think long-term, a skill that has served me well in both business and life.

Applying the Sacrifice Evaluation Framework: A Practical Exercise

To help you make strategic sacrifices in your own life, here's a simple exercise I use whenever I face a difficult choice: The Sacrifice Clarity Exercise. This exercise takes just a few minutes, but it can help you evaluate and commit to sacrifices that lead to long-term rewards.

Clarify Your Goal (2 Minutes): Write down one long-term goal you're working toward. Be specific, whether it's building a business, improving your health, or strengthening a relationship. For example: "I want to grow my business to support my family's future."

Weigh the Cost (2 Minutes): Identify one sacrifice you'll need to make to achieve that goal. What will you have to give up in the short term? Write down the cost and evaluate whether it's worth the reward. For example: "I'll need to give up weekends for the next six months to work on new projects. Is this worth the financial stability it will bring?"

Commit with Intention (1 Minute): Decide to make the sacrifice and write down one action you'll take to commit to it. For example: "I'll schedule my weekends for the next month to focus on new clients, and I'll plan a family outing next month to balance it out." Commit to taking that action within the next 24 hours.

I used this exercise when deciding to take on the school project. It helped me clarify my goal, weigh the cost of missing the vacation, and commit to the sacrifice with a plan to make it up to Sofia later. Try it for yourself. It's a powerful way to turn sacrifices into strategic investments in your future.

Conclusion: Sacrificing for a Legacy That Lasts

That school project was more than just a job it was a lesson in the power of sacrifice. It taught me that the choices we make, the things we give up, shape the structures of our lives. By sacrificing that vacation, I built a future for Sofia and myself a future of stability, opportunity, and shared memories. Sacrifice isn't about loss; it's about gain. It's about choosing to invest in the things that matter most, even when it means giving up something you value in the moment.

In construction, the strongest buildings often require the greatest investments of time, resources, and care. In life, the same is true. As you face your own choices, remember that every sacrifice you make is a brick in the foundation of your legacy. It builds a stronger future, deepens your commitment, teaches you what truly matters, creates exponential growth, and inspires those around you. Clarify your goals, weigh the costs, and commit with intention. When you do, you'll find that the things you give up today become the very things that build a future worth having a legacy that stands the test of time.

6

The Mindset of Ingenuity

"Do what you can, with what you have, where you are." Theodore
Roosevelt

Starting from scratch, whether it's after a failure, a setback, or
a new venture, is one of the most daunting yet transformative
experiences in both business and life. When you find yourself at
square one, like me, you're often faced with an overwhelming sense
of uncertainty and limited resources. But it is precisely in these
moments that the power of resourcefulness shines the brightest. It
is the defining trait that separates those who rise from those who
remain stagnant.

At my lowest point, I discovered something crucial: The power
to create, innovate, and rebuild lies not in the abundance of what
you have, but in your ability to make the most of what's at your
disposal.

This chapter is about transforming the challenging reality of
starting from scratch into an opportunity for profound growth.

How resourcefulness is not just a survival skill but a strategy for rebuilding your life and business from the ground up.

The Ingenuity Mindset: Turning Constraints into Opportunities

The builder's mindset uses resourcefulness, creativity, and the willingness to work with what you have. When I started rebuilding from zero, I didn't have much, just a small crew, a handful of tools, and a burning desire to create a better life for myself and my daughter. But I discovered that those limitations forced me to think differently, to find solutions I never would have considered otherwise.

Ingenuity is a skill that applies far beyond construction. It's a universal principle for anyone starting from scratch. The ingenuity mindset can help you turn constraints into opportunities. I've seen this in the lives of other builders and entrepreneurs over the years. A contractor I worked with once lost his entire inventory in a warehouse fire, but instead of giving up, he used salvaged materials to create a new line of custom furniture, turning a loss into a thriving business. A single mother I met started a catering business with just a small kitchen and a handful of recipes, using her creativity to build a loyal customer base. When you're starting from zero, ingenuity becomes your greatest asset.

The Power of Ingenuity: A Lesson from the Ashes

When I hit rock bottom after my divorce, I had to rebuild my life from scratch. I had lost my home, my savings were depleted, and my business was struggling to stay afloat. I couldn't afford to take on big projects; I barely had enough to pay my crew. But I knew I couldn't let my circumstances define me. I had to find a way to keep going, to rebuild with what I had.

One of my first projects during that time was a small repair job for a local farmer. He needed a barn fixed, but his budget was tight, and I didn't have the resources to buy new materials. I could have turned down the job, but I saw it as an opportunity to test my ingenuity. I walked around the farmer's property, looking for anything I could use. I found old wooden planks in a shed, rusted nails, and a pile of discarded stones that could be repurposed. With those materials, and a lot of creativity, I repaired the barn. It wasn't perfect, but it was functional, and the farmer was thrilled. That job didn't just pay my bills, it reminded me that even when you have nothing, you can still build something meaningful if you're willing to think differently.

That experience taught me the power of ingenuity. In construction, we often face constraints, like limited materials, tight budgets, or unexpected challenges. But a true builder doesn't see those constraints as barriers; they see them as opportunities to innovate. Ingenuity isn't just a skill it's a mindset, a way of looking at the world that says, "I can make this work with what I have." It's the ability to turn scarcity into abundance, to find solutions where others see only problems.

Repairing the barn wasn't just an act of ingenuity; it was a step toward rebuilding my confidence after the divorce. Every nail I straightened, every plank I repurposed, felt like a small victory, a reminder that I could rise again, even from nothing.

The Science of Ingenuity: How Creativity Drives Success

Ingenuity is a cognitive ability that can be cultivated. Scientists have found that creativity is linked to the brain's ability to make new connections between seemingly unrelated ideas, a process known as divergent thinking. When I repurposed those old planks and stones to fix the farmer's barn, my brain was engaging in divergent thinking, finding new uses for materials that others might have discarded. Research shows that divergent thinking is a key predictor of problem-solving success, and it's a skill that can be developed through practice.

Studies also show that constraints can actually boost creativity. When resources are limited, our brains are forced to think more innovatively, coming up with solutions we wouldn't have considered otherwise. This phenomenon, known as constraint-driven innovation, explains why some of the most groundbreaking ideas come from situations of scarcity. For me, the financial constraints after my divorce forced me to get creative, leading to solutions that not only kept my business alive but also set the stage for future growth.

The Ingenuity Framework: Building with What You Have

I have developed a way to help me use initiative when starting from zero: the Ingenuity Framework. This framework involves thinking creatively to make the most of what you have, even when it feels like you have nothing.

Assess – Take Stock of What You Have: The first step is to assess your resources, no matter how limited they seem. Look around. What do you have at your disposal? For me, this meant taking stock of the old planks, nails, and stones on that farmer's property. In your life, it might mean identifying your skills, your network, or even your time. Write down everything you have, no matter how small. The key is to see your resources with fresh eyes, recognizing their potential.

Adapt – Find Creative Solutions: Once you've assessed your resources, adapt them to fit your needs. This is where creativity comes in think outside the box to find new uses for what you have. For me, this meant using discarded stones to reinforce the barn's foundation and straightening rusted nails to save on costs. In your life, it might mean using a skill in a new way, repurposing an old idea, or finding a creative workaround for a problem. Ask yourself: How can I use what I have in a way I haven't before?

Apply – Put Your Plan into Action: The final step is to apply your creative solutions with intention. Take the resources you've adapted and put them to work, building something new. For me, this meant repairing the barn with the materials I had, creating a functional structure despite my limitations. In your life, it might mean launching a project with the skills you have, starting a side hustle with minimal resources, or rebuilding a relationship with the time you can offer. The goal is to create something meaningful, even if it's not perfect.

This process helped me rebuild from zero and turn scarcity into opportunity.

Applying the Ingenuity Framework: A Practical Exercise

To help you apply the ingenuity mindset in your own life, here's a simple exercise I use whenever I'm faced with limited resources: The Ingenuity Challenge. This exercise takes just a few minutes, but it can help you turn constraints into opportunities and start rebuilding from zero.

Assess (2 Minutes): Write down a current challenge you're facing where you feel limited by resources, whether it's time, money, skills, or materials. Then, list three resources you do have, no matter how small. For example: "I want to start a side business, but I lack funding. I have a laptop, a few hours a week, and a skill in graphic design."

Adapt (2 Minutes): Brainstorm one creative way to use each of those resources to address your challenge. Think outside the box. How can you repurpose what you have? For example: "I can use my laptop to create a portfolio online, my free hours to offer freelance design services, and my skill to design affordable logos for small businesses."

Apply (1 Minute): Choose one of your ideas and commit to taking a small, actionable step within the next 24 hours. For example: "I'll create a profile on a freelance platform tonight and offer my first design service."

I used this exercise when I took on that barn repair job with limited resources. It helped me see the potential in what I had and gave me the confidence to move forward. Try it for yourself. It's a powerful way to turn scarcity into a starting point for something new.

Beyond the Barn: Using Ingenuity

The Ingenuity Framework isn't limited to construction it can be applied to any challenge. A teacher with limited resources can assess their needs, adapt free tools, and apply them to create engaging lessons. A startup founder with a tight budget can assess their network, adapt by bartering services, and apply those connections to secure partnerships.

Ingenuity turns constraints into invitations to innovate.

Conclusion: Building from Zero with Ingenuity

That small repair job for the farmer wasn't just a project, it was a profound lesson in the power of ingenuity. It taught me that starting from zero isn't a limitation; it's an opportunity to think differently, to create with what you have, and to build something meaningful from the ground up. The builder's mindset doesn't wait for the perfect conditions or the right resources it uses what's in front of you, no matter how little, to lay the foundation for something greater.

So, if you find yourself at square one, remember this: Ingenuity is not just a skill, it's a superpower. You are not defined by what you lack. You are defined by what you do with what you have. Every small step you take, every creative solution you find, every obstacle you overcome are the building blocks of your new foundation. They are proof that you have the power to rise, to rebuild, and to create a life of purpose and meaning.

So, take a deep breath, roll up your sleeves, and start building. The world is waiting for what you will create. And remember, no matter how small your resources may seem, they are more than enough to begin. Because the greatest resource you have is not outside of you, it's within you. It's your ingenuity, your determination, and your unwavering belief that you can make something meaningful out of what you have.

This is the builder's mindset. This is the path to rebuilding from zero. And this is your moment to rise.

7

The Power of Staying Humble

"Docendo discimus." "By teaching, we learn." Seneca

On the path to success, there is one element that is often overlooked or forgotten: humility. In a world that glorifies individualism and the desire to stand out, staying humble may seem like a difficult task. However, true strength lies in the ability to keep our feet on the ground, even when we achieve great milestones. Being humble does not mean abandoning our achievements, but rather recognizing that these successes are the result of shared efforts, moments of growth, and constant improvement. Humility is not just a moral virtue but a practice that allows us to remain grounded and focused, even when we reach the highest peaks.

Humility as the Foundation of Growth

Humility is the foundation upon which every growth journey is built. Without humility, there is no openness to improvement. Every person, regardless of the level of success achieved, has areas for growth. Humble people know that learning never stops. Every sacrifice, every mistake, every new experience is an opportunity to become a better version of oneself. A humble person doesn't feel threatened by the success of others, but instead celebrates and learns from others' experiences and results, recognizing that everyone has something unique to offer. Humility, then, is the gateway to personal growth, because it allows us to admit that there is always something to improve and that every new experience is a lesson.

Never Losing Sight of Your Roots

As we progress toward success, it's easy to become overwhelmed by the results we achieve and forget where we started. Our roots represent the foundation that allowed us to grow and reach where we are today. Humility helps us remember who we are and where we came from, keeping us anchored in reality. No matter how high we rise, if we forget our origins, we risk losing sight of what got us here. Staying humble means honoring our past, our experiences, and the people who supported us along the way. Our roots remind us that success does not rely simply on talent or ability, but on determination, sacrifice, and the support received along the journey. When we keep our roots in mind, we can face future challenges with greater serenity, knowing that every step forward is the result of a journey that deserves to be appreciated.

Humility in Relationships

Relationships are one of the most important aspects of life. Humility has a profound impact on our relationships with others, whether family, friends, or colleagues. When we are humble, we are willing to question ourselves, apologize when we are wrong, and recognize the value of others. Humility makes us more open to listening and more inclined to offer support. A person who feels superior to others will hardly be able to build strong and sincere relationships. Humility fosters mutual respect, understanding, and trust. Every relationship is a two-way street: giving and receiving, supporting and being supported. Humility in relationships helps us build lasting connections and has a positive impact on the people around us, creating an environment of collaboration and respect.

Humility as Strength

Many people believe that humility is a form of weakness, but in reality, it is one of the strongest qualities a person can possess. Humility makes us more resilient because it allows us to face difficulties not with arrogance, but with determination and an open mind. A humble person knows that challenges are part of the journey and that every difficulty is an opportunity for growth. Humility pushes us to never give up, to never be too proud to ask for help, or to admit that we still have more to learn. Humility does not make us passive: it teaches us to work with others, to build bridges, and to seek solutions not for our own ego, but for the greater good. True strength does not lie in forcefulness or arrogance, but in the ability to remain calm, focused, and respectful of others while working constantly to improve.

The Power to Inspire

Humility has the power to inspire others. A humble person does not present themselves as an example of perfection, but as an example of determination and growth. When we see someone who has achieved great results but remains humble and open, we are more likely to follow them, to learn from them, and to try to emulate their behavior. Humble leadership is the form of leadership that has the greatest impact. This type of leader knows that their success is the result of teamwork and never takes credit for others' contributions. They inspire others to do the same, creating a culture of collaboration, respect, and growth. Humility is not just a quality that enriches the person who possesses it; it is also a powerful tool that can motivate and inspire others to pursue their dreams and continually improve.

The Risk of Losing Humility

Success is a double-edged sword. On one hand, it can be the reward for hard work and sacrifice; on the other, it can cause us to lose sight of humility. The risk of becoming arrogant or feeling superior to others is always present when we reach important milestones. However, it is precisely in these moments that we must be particularly vigilant. Success should never become a reason to detach from reality or to lord over others. A leader who loses humility risks isolating themselves, losing the ability to inspire others, and compromising their own opportunities. Being aware of this risk helps us protect humility not as a passive virtue, but as an active force that guides us on our journey.

Humility and Gratitude

Humility and gratitude go hand in hand. When we are humble, we recognize that everything we have achieved is the result of a journey made possible by the support of others and favorable circumstances. Gratitude allows us to appreciate every step we've taken, without ever taking it for granted or being superior. Being grateful for what we have helps us maintain a healthy and realistic perspective, understanding that we are not alone in our journey. At the same time, gratitude helps us stay motivated and continue giving our best, ensuring that every step toward success is accompanied by a deep respect for the process and the people who have helped along the way.

Conclusion

I learnt to be humble when I returned to my father's home after my failed marriage and struggling business. I had to accept that I had more to learn. I soon saw that remaining humble didn't diminish my previous accomplishments; but made me grateful for the journey that brought me to that point.

It is essential to appreciate the experiences, challenges, and lessons learned along the way. Humility allows us to see beyond our own achievements and acknowledge that we are part of something much larger than ourselves. It reminds us that every step we take, every victory we experience, is intertwined with the help and support of those around us, be it family, friends, colleagues, or mentors. Recognizing this interconnectedness fosters a sense of gratitude, strong relationships, and inspiration. It encourages a mindset that is not centered on the self, but on the collective effort involved.

Humility is, in fact, a profound strength. It empowers us to grow continuously because it fosters an openness to learning and adapting. Staying humble means accepting that no one is above mistakes, no one is above growth, and no one is above the need for others. It allows us to stay connected to our roots and the people who helped shape our journey.

PART TWO

THE INTERNAL STRUCTURE: BUILDING MINDSET AND CHARACTER

8

The Power of Vision: Thinking Like a Builder

"Vision is the art of seeing what is invisible to others." Jonathan
Swift

In the world of construction, the true builder doesn't simply
look at raw materials like wood, stone, or steel. A true builder
visualizes the completed structure before the first brick is even laid.
They see the entire building, down to the finest detail: how the
light will filter through the windows, how the rooms will flow
together, and how the structure will stand as a testament to design
and craftsmanship. This ability to visualize, to see a future reality
before it exists, is what sets apart the visionary from the rest of the
crowd.

A visionary can see what others cannot. They understand that
every dream, project, and enterprise starts with a clear, focused
picture. They can see the outcome of their efforts before they start.

This chapter will explore the profound power of vision, and how thinking like a builder can shape your future.

The Mind of a Builder: A Vision Before Action

Before any building rises from the ground, it exists in the mind of the builder. They know exactly what it will look like, how it will function, and even the way it will feel to those who walk through it. The architect doesn't simply draw a plan—they envision a future in which the building will serve a purpose, enhance the landscape, and become a landmark.

Creative thinkers prepare for obstacles and remain focused on the end goal, even when the path ahead seems unclear.

But vision alone is not enough. A visionary must be able to communicate this vision to others. In the world of construction, this is done through detailed plans, drawings, and models. In life, this is done through leadership, persuasive communication, and inspiring others to share in the dream. Without this ability to articulate and share your vision, it can remain nothing more than an idea in your mind. To build the future, you need the ability to make others see it too.

Visionaries See Beyond the Present

To be a visionary is to see not just what is, but what could be. While most people are often confined to their current circumstances, visionaries think beyond their present environment. They look ahead, often to a future that others may not see, and it is this foresight that allows them to lead change and make a lasting impact.

Consider the example of Arnold Schwarzenegger. While many knew him as a bodybuilder, he envisioned himself as an actor, businessman, and even a politician long before those dreams became reality. He didn't let his humble beginnings or the skepticism of others hold him back. His vision drove him to constantly evolve and reinvent himself. His success was the result of the clarity with which he saw his future.

Another example is Steve Jobs, whose vision for Apple wasn't just about creating computers, it was about transforming how people interacted with technology. Jobs didn't just see gadgets; he saw the future of personal computing, the digital revolution, and an interconnected world. His ability to see these possibilities, when most people couldn't, allowed him to change the world in ways that seemed impossible at the time.

In both cases, these visionaries saw beyond the present. They didn't get bogged down by the limitations of their current reality; instead, they focused on the potential that lay ahead. Their vision wasn't just about achieving success, it was about reshaping the world around them. They understood that success is born from a commitment to a long-term vision, not a short-term goal.

Visionaries Build a Blueprint for Success

When a builder starts a project, they begin with a blueprint, a detailed plan that outlines the structure, design, and sequence of construction. This blueprint serves as both a guide and a measurement of success. Every step taken in the construction process follows the vision laid out in the original plan.

In life and business, your vision is your blueprint. It's not enough to have a vague idea of what you want to achieve. Visionaries are specific. They create a clear picture of their future, and they break it down into actionable steps.

Similarly, you must create a blueprint for your life. This plan must be clear, detailed, and specific. Start with your ultimate goal, but then break it down. What steps will you take to reach it? What obstacles will you face along the way, and how will you overcome them? Having a clear, actionable plan makes your vision tangible. It turns your dreams into measurable objectives.

For example, Elon Musk didn't just wake up one day and decide to send a rocket to Mars. He had a long-term vision and a detailed plan for SpaceX years of research, development, testing, and building. He knew the obstacles that lay ahead and he made a blueprint for overcoming them. His unwavering belief in his vision allowed him to push through the failures and setbacks, ultimately making space exploration more accessible than ever before.

Visionaries Build a Circle of Support

One crucial aspect of becoming a visionary is surrounding yourself with the right people. The company you keep plays a significant role in either supporting or hindering your ability to realize your vision. Don't listen to people who drag you down. There will always be individuals who doubt you, discourage you, or make you feel small. These voices, if allowed to remain, can cloud your vision and slow your progress.

Visionaries often thrive by learning from others who have walked the same path and faced similar challenges. They don't allow the negativity of others to shape their perspective. Instead, they remain focused on their goals and choose to collaborate with people who inspire, motivate, and help them see possibilities beyond what they initially imagined.

Change your crowd seek out people who believe in your potential, who challenge you to grow, and who support your vision.. Success is not a solo journey, and the people around you can either propel you forward or keep you stuck in a place of mediocrity.

The Role of Vision in Overcoming Challenges

Visionaries are not immune to challenges. In fact, the road to success is often filled with obstacles, doubts, and setbacks. But what sets visionaries apart is their ability to remain focused on their end goal, despite the difficulties they face. They understand that challenges are a natural part of the process, and that success is never achieved without perseverance.

Take Elon Musk, again. His vision for Tesla, SpaceX, and the future of sustainable energy has transformed industries and changed the world. But it hasn't been without its challenges. Musk has faced numerous setbacks; failed rockets, financial difficulties, and skepticism from critics. Yet, his unwavering belief in his vision has propelled him forward, turning impossible ideas into reality.

Visionaries possess resilience. They understand that failure is not a permanent state, but a stepping-stone toward eventual success. They learn from their mistakes, adapt their strategies, and continue to push forward.

The Legacy of Visionaries

The impact of visionary individuals is profound and enduring. The buildings, companies, and ideas created by visionaries leave a lasting legacy that shapes the world for generations to come. Think of the iconic structures built by visionary architects or the companies that have redefined entire industries. These achievements were made possible by individuals who had the foresight to see beyond the present and take action to create the future.

The Building Blocks of Visionary Thinking

Becoming a visionary requires a mindset shift. It's about seeing the big picture and understanding that the journey from where you are to where you want to be doesn't happen overnight. Visionaries are not afraid to dream big, but they also understand that every great achievement is made up of small, strategic steps. Below are the key building blocks of visionary thinking:

Clarity of Purpose: A true visionary knows exactly what they are trying to achieve. They have a crystal-clear sense of their mission and goals. This clarity serves as their North Star, guiding their actions and decisions. Without clarity, you risk wandering aimlessly, reacting to the world instead of shaping it.

Imagination and Creativity: Visionaries are not constrained by the limitations of the present moment. They use their creativity to imagine a world different from the one they see today. This imagination is a powerful tool that allows them to solve problems in innovative ways and create something unique. They challenge the status quo and find new paths where others see only obstacles.

Commitment to Action: Vision alone is not enough. Visionaries are driven to take action. They transform their ideas into reality by staying committed, even in the face of setbacks or failures. Their belief in their vision pushes them to keep moving forward, regardless of the obstacles. Action is the bridge between vision and reality.

Adaptability and Flexibility: The path to achieving a vision is rarely linear. Visionaries know that success requires adaptability. They are open to new ideas, solutions, and approaches. This flexibility allows them to overcome challenges and refine their vision as they go. They remain committed to the goal, but they are willing to change tactics when necessary.

Leadership and Inspiration: Visionaries don't work in isolation. They are leaders who inspire others to join them in their mission. Their vision becomes a shared dream that motivates and unites others, helping them work toward a common goal. Visionaries are often the catalysts for change, guiding others to see what is possible.

Resilience: Visionaries understand that obstacles are part of the journey. They are resilient in the face of failure, seeing it not as a defeat, but as an opportunity to learn and grow. When things don't go as planned, they adapt, improve, and press forward, undeterred by the challenges they encounter.

Conclusion: Building More Than Structures

Construction has taught me far more than how to build buildings. It's taught me how to build resilience, leadership, and problem-solving skills. It's taught me how to plan for success and how to navigate challenges. It's taught me to take a holistic, 360-degree view of everything I do, ensuring that every piece fits together to create something greater than the sum of its parts.

To be a visionary is to possess the rare ability to see what others cannot, to have the clarity to define your goals, the creativity to imagine new possibilities, and the commitment to turn your vision into reality. Like a builder with a blueprint in hand, you must have a clear vision of your future and take actionable steps to bring it to life.

In your own life, you have the power to be a visionary. Whether in your career, relationships, or personal growth, your vision can be the catalyst for change. When you think like a builder visualizing every detail of the project before it begins, you empower yourself to build a future that aligns with your greatest aspirations. The world is built by visionaries, and with the right mindset, you can be one of them.

9

Taming the Mind: From Fear to Action

"Courage is not the absence of fear, but the triumph over it."
Nelson Mandela

There is only one thing in this world that you can truly control
your mind.

From birth, we are conditioned to believe that life is an
uncontrollable force, that fate, luck, and external events govern
our existence. In response, we act with caution, allowing fear to
seep in and undermine our foundations. Most people operate like
abandoned construction sites–half-built, disorganized, overtaken
by weeds of doubt, fear, and distraction. They let the past haunt
them, the future terrify them, and the opinions of others shape
their reality. It is never their fault, blaming the weather, the traffic,
the market, their neighbor. They wait for the world to provide
stability instead of laying their own foundation. Ultimately, they
fail not because they are weak, but because they refuse to take

control of their own mental landscape. They are simply avoiding responsibility for the one thing they were always meant to master.

It doesn't have to be this way. The mind is not some mystical entity beyond our reach. It is a tool, a system to be built and refined, just as a builder shapes a masterpiece from raw materials. You are the architect of your mind. You either design it with precision, or you let it crumble under the weight of external chaos and fear.

The mind is the ultimate tool, the foundation upon which every decision, action, and outcome is built. If you do not control it, it will control you. It will amplify your fears, distort your perceptions, and sabotage your potential. But if you master it, it becomes your greatest ally, a source of clarity, resilience, and unwavering focus.

This chapter explores the strategic process of confronting personal and professional fears, turning doubt into determination, and taking action despite uncertainty. Fear and doubt aren't enemies to be eradicated, but challenges that can be transformed into stepping stones for growth.

The Enemy Within

Your worst enemy is not outside of you. It is not time, not failure, not other people. Your worst enemy is the untrained mind. One that is undisciplined, unfocused, easily swayed by every passing emotion and circumstance. It's the mind that reacts instead of deciding with intention and clinging to comfort instead of growth.

It's the voice that tells you, *You are not ready. You are not capable. You will fail.* It's the voice of fear.

This enemy is subtle. It does not attack with force, but with whispers. It convinces you that you are powerless, that the world is against you, that success is reserved for others. It feeds on your doubts, your fears, your insecurities. And if you let it, it will consume you.

But here is the truth: this enemy is only as powerful as you allow it to be. Like an unskilled builder who blames the storm for a weak foundation, the undisciplined mind blames life for its struggles. But the storm is not the problem, the foundation is. And the foundation is your responsibility.

In construction, every project comes with risks, be it a structural failure, a missed deadline, or an unhappy client. In life, the risks are just as real: the fear of failure, the doubt that you're not good enough, the uncertainty of stepping into the unknown. To overcome these challenges, we first need to understand them.

The Anatomy of Fear and Doubt

Fear and doubt are universal experiences; shadows that lurk in the corners of every human being's mind, whether you're constructing a physical structure or a life of purpose. Overcoming fear and doubt isn't having willpower. It's understanding how your brain works and using that knowledge to your advantage. Scientists have found that we can rewire our brains to respond differently through intentional practice.

Fear is a survival mechanism deeply rooted in our biology. It's regulated by the amygdala, a part of the brain that triggers the "fight or flight" response. When we face uncertainty, the amygdala signals danger, even if the threat isn't real. This mechanism, useful in life-or-death situations, often overreacts in modern life, treating every uncertainty as a potential catastrophe.

Example: Imagine walking on a suspended walkway hundreds of meters above the ground. Even though you're safe, your brain warns you of danger, activating fear. This is the amygdala in action, a system designed to protect you, but one that can also hold you back if left unchecked.

Doubt, on the other hand, is the voice of insecurity, a byproduct of fear that questions our abilities and worth. Together, fear and doubt create a powerful barrier, stopping us from taking the risks necessary for growth.

A Defining Moment

In the early 2000s, my construction business was at a crossroads. I had built a solid reputation for small residential projects, but I wanted to take on larger, more complex commercial projects, contracts that would elevate my company to a new level. An opportunity came in the form of a bid for a large community center in Sassari, a project that would require twice the resources, manpower, and expertise of anything I had tackled before. It was the kind of project I had always dreamed of, but as I prepared the bid, doubt began to creep in.

I was plagued by questions: Was I ready for a project of this scale? What if I failed to deliver and damaged my reputation? What if I overextended my resources and bankrupted my company? The fear was palpable. I was afraid of failure, afraid of the unknown, afraid of losing everything I had worked so hard to build. Every night, I wrestled with these doubts, my mind racing with worst-case scenarios. I nearly backed out of the bid, convinced that I wasn't ready, that I wasn't good enough.

But then, I remembered a lesson my grandfather taught me as a child while we were repairing a crumbling wall on our family's property. I had been hesitant to climb the rickety ladder to fix the upper stones, afraid I might fall. He looked at me and said in Sardinian, "CASTIA E IMPARA"–watch and learn. He climbed the ladder himself, showing me that the fear of falling didn't have to stop me; I just had to take one careful step at a time. That memory gave me the clarity I needed. I couldn't let fear and doubt stop me from taking a step forward. I submitted the bid, and to my surprise, I won the contract.

The community center project wasn't easy. It came with its share of challenges, from tight deadlines to unexpected structural issues, but I faced each obstacle with a newfound determination. Winning that contract and completing the project taught me that fear and doubt don't have to be barriers; they can be the fuel that drives you to grow, to take risks, and to achieve more than you ever thought possible.

That realization was a turning point for me. I had to learn to let go of the illusion of control and focus on mastering my mindset instead.

Mastering the Mind

To control your mind is to control your reality. This is not philosophy; this is a fundamental truth. If you build mental strength, no event, no person, no external circumstance can dictate your fate. The world may be chaotic, but you will remain unshaken. The market may collapse, but you will adapt. People may betray you, but you will not break. You will not be controlled, but the one who controls.

Mastery of the mind does not mean you suppress emotions or pretend that challenges do not exist. Instead, it is developing the clarity to see reality as it is, the discipline to act with intention, and the resilience to persist despite setbacks. It is building a mental framework that allows you to navigate chaos with calm and purpose. There is no great mystery here, no hidden knowledge that only a few possess. You already know this truth. You have always known it. But knowing is not enough. You must act. Your mind must be strong, disciplined, and unshakable, like a fortress. You must choose whether you will remain at the mercy of the world or take control of the one thing that has always been yours.

You are the builder. You are the architect. And the structure you are building is your mind.

Practical Steps to Master your Mind

Step 1: Acknowledge – Face the Fear

The first step is to pay attention to your thoughts. Notice when your mind is sabotaging you with doubt, fear, or negativity. Don't try to ignore them or push them away; instead, name them. For me, this meant admitting that I was afraid of failing on the community center project, afraid of not being good enough. Acknowledging the fear takes away its power, making it something you can address rather than something that controls you.

Exercise: Write down one fear or doubt that's holding you back right now. Be specific.

Step 2: Analyze – Separate Fact from Fiction

Fear often exaggerates reality, turning possibilities into certainties. When a negative thought arises, challenge it. Analyze your fear by separating fact from fiction. Ask yourself: Is this true? Is this helpful? Replace it with a thought that empowers you. What's the worst that could happen? Is it as bad as your mind makes it out to be? For me, the worst-case scenario was failing the project and losing my reputation, but I realized that even if that happened, I could rebuild. By analyzing the fear, I saw

This is known as **Cognitive Reframing.** Instead of seeing fear as a sign to stop, reframe it as a sign of growth. Studies show that reframing fear as excitement can reduce its negative impact and improve performance.

Exercise: Break down your fear. What's the worst that could happen? How likely is it?

Step 3: Act – Take One Step Forward

The best way to overcome fear and doubt is through action. Take one small, actionable step toward your goal, even if it feels uncomfortable. For me, this meant submitting the bid for the community center project, despite my doubts. That single step broke the cycle of fear and gave me the momentum I needed to keep going. Action doesn't have to be perfect, it just has to be forward motion.

Once you have taken one action, build a routine. Just as a builder follows a blueprint, create a daily routine that supports mental clarity and focus. Set small, daily goals that require mental focus and follow through. Whether it's waking up early, meditating, or completing a task without distraction, discipline builds mental strength. Include practices like journaling, exercise, and mindfulness.

Exercise: Identify one small step you can take today to confront your fear.

Step 4: Embrace Discomfort

Growth happens outside your comfort zone. Take on challenges that scare you and use them as opportunities to strengthen your mind. Use **gradual exposure.** Face your fears in small, manageable doses. By starting with smaller risks, you build the confidence needed to tackle bigger challenges.

Exercise: Identify something that will take you out of your comfort zone. What is one some action that could nudge you into that?

Conclusion: Turning Fear and Doubt into Fuel for Success

In construction, every project comes with risks, but the greatest risk is letting fear and doubt stop you from building the future you envision. The community center project was a defining moment in my career, not because it was my biggest success, but because it taught me how to confront fear and doubt head-on by mastering my mind. Every great builder knows that the foundation is everything. Without a solid base, even the most beautiful structure will crumble under pressure. Your mind is no different. It is the foundation upon which your life is built. If it is weak, disorganized, or neglected, everything else will falter. But if it is strong, disciplined, and carefully constructed, it can withstand any storm. You have everything you need to build a mind that is unshakable. Discipline is your hammer. Clarity is your level. Focus is your blueprint. These tools are not reserved for the privileged or the gifted. They are available to anyone willing to pick them up and put in the work.

I learned that fear isn't a barrier to success; it's a signal to take action. Doubt isn't a sign of failure; it's an opportunity to grow. By acknowledging, analyzing, and acting on my fears, I turned uncertainty into a catalyst for achievement. As you face your own fears, personal or professional, remember that courage isn't the absence of fear; it's the decision to act despite it. Use fear and doubt as tools to drive you forward, one step at a time, until you've built a foundation strong enough to withstand any challenge.

10

The Power of Self-Care: Forging Body and Mind for Success

"*Mens sana in corpore sano.*" "A healthy mind in a healthy body."
Decimus Junius Juvenalis

As a leader, you are constantly under pressure: tight deadlines, increasing demands, competition, and responsibilities that require your maximum energy. In this context, it's easy to neglect your well-being, considering it a luxury or something secondary to work. However, experience has taught me that self-care is not optional it's a necessity. The success of your work depends on your ability to maintain a balance between body and mind. Neglecting this aspect not only compromises your performance but also undermines the very foundation of your work and your team. A healthy and strong body not only allows you to face daily challenges with more energy but also directly impacts your ability to make better decisions, especially in the business world. In a competitive environment, the right decisions can be the difference between success and failure. That's why physical training and maintaining a healthy body are crucial factors for any entrepreneur or professional looking to achieve peak performance.

The Cost of Neglect: A Lesson Learned the Hard Way

Early in my career, I made the mistake of sacrificing everything in the name of work. I believed that sleeping little, eating poorly, and ignoring the signals from my body were signs of dedication and resilience. I managed ten construction sites simultaneously, neglected my family, and thought I was invincible. But reality hit me with an uncomfortable truth: working nonstop didn't make me stronger–it brought me to the brink of collapse.

Exhaustion compromised my ability to make clear decisions. My concentration waned, my creativity dried up, and my team suffered from my lack of energy. Burnout became a constant presence: chronic fatigue, irritability, difficulty sleeping, and a sense of emptiness. I wasn't leading; I was surviving, and my business was paying the price.

That experience taught me a fundamental lesson: I am the cornerstone of my work. If my body and mind are not in shape, the entire system suffers. Self-care is not a waste of time it's an investment in success. From that moment on, I decided to change my approach, transforming my routine to build a solid foundation from which to operate.

A Strong and Trained Body for Better Business Decisions

Decision-making is a daily task in business: from resource management and strategy planning to problem-solving and negotiation. In the business world, every decision can have a huge impact. When we're physically fit, our minds are clearer and better able to analyze information logically. Similarly, physical exercise stimulates the production of endorphins, which improve our mood and reduce anxiety, creating an ideal mental state for handling even the most stressful situations. A healthy body not only gives us the physical energy to handle a long day of work.

A Healthy Body Reduces Uncertainty and Helps Manage Risk in Business

In business, risk management is essential. Uncertainty is a constant, but a strong and healthy body helps us stay calm and clear-headed even in turbulent times. Confidence in oneself, born from feeling healthy, translates into a greater ability to handle risks and make effective business choices without being paralyzed by difficulties.

An entrepreneur who works out regularly is better prepared to face business challenges with resilience, much like an athlete preparing for a tough race. Physical and mental strength allows for better management of periods of intense pressure, improving not only the quality of work but also the ability to respond positively to any unforeseen events.

The Pillars of Self-Care: Balancing Body and Mind

To maintain a sustainable balance, I've identified four fundamental pillars that are essential for both personal well-being and professional success:

1. Physical Exercise: Physical activity is a powerful tool for managing stress and maintaining high energy levels. You don't need to become an athlete: just 30 minutes a day of walking, running, or gym training can improve your mood, increase concentration, and reduce anxiety. Personally, I find that a morning run or a weightlifting session helps me start the day with a clear mind. Exercise isn't just about staying fit, it's an ally for productivity and mental clarity.

2. Nutrition: Food is the fuel for your body and mind. A balanced diet, rich in lean proteins, whole grains, vegetables, and healthy fats (like omega-3s from fish), improves concentration, mood, and physical stamina. Avoiding processed foods and refined sugars is crucial for maintaining high energy levels throughout the day. I've learned to plan my meals, prioritizing nutritious foods that provide lasting energy rather than resorting to quick but unhealthy options.

3. Hydration: Drinking enough water is a simple but often overlooked habit. Dehydration can cause fatigue, headaches, and difficulty concentrating. I've started keeping a water bottle on my desk and monitoring how much I drink during the day. It's a small adjustment that makes a big difference.

4. Sleep: Getting at least 7-8 hours of sleep per night is essential for physical and mental recovery. Lack of sleep impairs decision-making, creativity, and stress management. I've learned to respect my sleep-wake cycle, avoiding work in bed and creating an evening routine that helps me relax.

Practical Strategies for Integrating Self-Care

I've talked a lot here about looking after the physical body, but self-care is also needed for the mind and emotions. Here are some strategies I've adopted to make mental health an integral part of my routine:

1. Set Boundaries: I've learned to say no and define my time. Work emails and calls no longer invade my evenings or weekends. This allows me to recharge and return to work with more energy. Setting clear boundaries between work and personal life is essential to avoid burnout.

2. Make Time for Yourself: I dedicate at least 30 minutes a

day to exercise and try to eat mindfully, avoiding work during meals. This time is non-negotiable: it's a fixed appointment with myself.

3. Ask for Help: Delegating and relying on competent team members is not a sign of weakness, but a sign of intelligence. I've surrounded myself with trusted people to whom I can delegate tasks, freeing up time and energy to focus on priorities.

4. Seek Support: Talking to a mentor, coach, or therapist can provide new perspectives and tools for managing stress. There's no need to be afraid to ask for help when needed. I've found great value in consulting professionals who help me reflect and improve my approach to work and life.

5. Practice Mindfulness: Techniques like meditation or simply dedicating a few minutes a day to deep breathing can help reduce stress and improve concentration. You don't need to be an expert: just a few minutes a day can make a difference.

Conclusion: Training to Achieve Success in Business

The importance of having a healthy and strong body and mind in business cannot be overstated. A trained and fit body is the foundation that allows for clearer, more rational, and advantageous decisions, reducing the risk of errors caused by fatigue or stress. The synergy between body and mind is the real engine that drives success in business because only when we are able to manage our physical well-being can we also manage our mental well-being and make informed decisions. Entrepreneurs and professionals who invest in their physical health not only improve the quality of their lives, but they also increase their chances of success in business. In a world where every decision matters, a strong and healthy body is the key to facing challenges with determination, strategy, and clarity an investment that pays off in the long term, leading to wiser decisions and a prosperous career.

Remember: you are the engine of your success. Take care of yourself, and everything else will follow.

11

Self-Awareness: The Foundation of Success

"The foundations of every state are the education of its youth."
Diogenes

A building is only as solid as its foundations, and the same applies to life and business. Without a solid foundation, nothing can withstand the test of time. Throughout my journey, I learned that the foundations of success are not just technical skills or hard work: they are self-awareness, discipline, and a clear sense of purpose. These are the pillars that support everything else.

The Importance of Solid Foundations

When I started my journey, I had the technical skills gained from years of experience in construction, but I still didn't fully understand how crucial it was to have a foundation in life. Just like a building starts with a plan and a stable ground, I too had to build my inner base, rooted in self-awareness, discipline, and a clear purpose.In my early twenties, I was completely focused on "doing." I was driven by ambition, but I didn't yet understand the deeper meaning of my actions. I lived day by day, focused on the next project, the next challenge, but not on what I truly wanted in life. It was then that I began to understand: without clear foundations, everything I built would collapse under its own weight.

Self-Awareness: The Starting Point

Self-awareness is not an abstract or spiritual concept: it is a strategic, concrete, and measurable skill. It is the ability to analyze oneself with clarity, without excuses or illusions. It means recognizing our mental patterns, automatic reactions, irrational fears, and the deep motivations that drive every choice we make.In a world where everyone chases results, status, or approval, true strength lies in stopping, observing, and understanding. Because only those who truly know themselves can make consistent decisions, build effective strategies, and lead with authority. Without self-awareness, every success is unstable. It's like building on sand: it may hold up for a while, but sooner or later, it will collapse.For years, I identified with my results: completed projects, goals achieved, challenges won. But that was only the surface. The turning point came when I began asking myself the fundamental questions: Why do I do what I do? What am I really seeking? What mechanisms sabotage me, even when everything seems to be going well?And the answers weren't always comfortable. But they were true.Self-awareness is the starting point. It is the foundation of any lasting transformation. Without it, we stumble forward, driven by chance or emotions. With it, every step becomes intentional. It's what sets the leader apart from the reactive person, the strategic entrepreneur from the mere operator.Someone truly aware doesn't chase: they build. They don't react: they choose. They don't hide: they act with clarity.And in a constantly changing world, self-awareness is not just a competitive advantage. It is the only real starting point for building something that lasts.

The Practice of Self-Awareness

Self-awareness is not a static goal, but a continuous and dynamic process. It is a daily exercise that offers no breaks, requiring constant vigilance and deliberate effort. It's not a momentary enlightenment, but an ongoing process of evaluation and reflection that adapts to life's changes and challenges. The practice of self-awareness begins with the ability to observe. Observing our thoughts, reactions, actions, and motivations without judgment, but with intellectual curiosity allows us to separate emotions from decisions. Every day is an opportunity to examine how we acted, how we faced difficulties, and which inner dynamics guided our choices. In some cases, this reflection may arise informally, such as in keeping an evening journal, where we question the effectiveness of our actions. Other times, awareness arrives more directly and sometimes uncomfortably: through external feedback, especially that which challenges our ego and forces us to confront uncomfortable truths. These moments of friction are crucial for improvement, as they reveal what we'd often prefer to ignore.

Self-awareness is not just understanding what we do, but also perceiving the forces that guide us. It requires the ability to recognize when our actions are driven by ego, when our choices are influenced by fear, or when we are operating automatically without conscious control. It is a practice that pushes us to question our reaction to external factors and recognize when we act to please or avoid conflict rather than aligning with deeper, more consistent values. This practice is not always simple or pleasant. It requires courage and a willingness to face our weaknesses and inconsistencies. However, the result of this continuous process is mental clarity. Clarity is not only the result of greater self-awareness, but it becomes a powerful tool for navigating a complex and constantly changing world. When we are aware of our motivations and inner dynamics, we can make better choices, make more informed decisions, and act with greater effectiveness. Clarity allows us to develop a clear and objective vision, which is the foundation of every conscious action. Ultimately, self-awareness is power. It is the power to consciously choose how to react to events, to act with consistency and determination, and to avoid being driven by external impulses or fleeting emotions. Without this power, we are vulnerable to external events and forces we don't understand. But with awareness, we can build our reality in a decisive, aligned, and responsible way.

Self-Awareness and Discipline: Preparing the Ground

As I grew and faced personal and professional challenges, I began to understand the importance of self-awareness. To truly build a successful life, I first had to understand who I was, what I valued, and where I wanted to go. This awareness didn't come overnight. It took years of trial, error, and reflection to discover what truly guided me and what really mattered to me. The journey was essential in this process. When I left Italy and began to explore the world, I started seeing everything with different eyes. I traveled to Africa, South America, and other places, each with its own culture, lifestyle, and approach to challenges. The diversity in how people lived and viewed the world forced me to rethink my perspective. In Africa, for example, I saw a life deeply different from the frantic, success-oriented life I was used to. The people I met didn't have the technological comforts or wealth I knew, but they possessed something far more valuable: a deep sense of purpose, resilience, and community spirit. Their lives were not based on material success, but on relationships, ingenuity, and the ability to give meaning to what they had. This experience opened my eyes and made me reflect on my life. I understood that to build something lasting; the foundation had to rest not only on external success but on inner clarity. It wasn't enough to work hard to achieve external goals. I had to anchor my life in awareness, discipline, and, above all, purpose. The more I traveled and absorbed different perspectives, the more I realized that building a meaningful life requires a deep understanding of oneself and a commitment to live with intention.

Purpose: The Heart of Long-Term Success

Purpose is the fundamental element that gives direction and stability to long-term success. Without a clear purpose, any achievement is hollow, and what is built risks being fragile and easily dismantled. True success is not measured solely by economic results or the appearance of achievement, but by the solidity that comes from pursuing a goal that has intrinsic and lasting value. Over the years, my experience has allowed me to fully understand the meaning of this notion. Through travel, interacting with different cultures, and facing professional challenges, I progressively clarified my purpose. I understood that my commitment to the construction industry, the companies I had created, and everything I had achieved were not ends in themselves, but part of an overarching vision that aimed at something greater: to contribute significantly not only to my own well-being but also to that of the people I worked with, my family, and the community I was part of. This discovery process was essential for transforming my work into a contribution that went beyond mere material success, projecting it toward a deeper, more lasting dimension. In the years that followed, the accumulated experiences allowed me to redefine and strengthen my purpose. I understood that it was no longer just about building physical structures or achieving financial success. My purpose evolved toward creating a legacy based on higher values such as integrity, personal and professional growth, and inspiring others to pursue their own path with determination and consistency. This purpose was no longer linked to a visible result, but rather to the quality of daily actions and the ability to transmit those principles through every aspect of my business and life. This clarity about my purpose represented the foundation upon which I was able to build every new project, face every challenge, and overcome obstacles. It was no longer about avoiding difficulties, but recognizing in every new experience an opportunity to align further with my values. Every step I take, every decision I make, is guided by this purpose, which provides me not only with motivation but also the resilience needed to overcome moments of uncertainty. Having a clear purpose, indeed, is what allows you to face the long term with stability. Difficulties are no longer seen as unforeseen events to avoid, but as an integral part of an evolutionary process that contributes to achieving a greater goal. Success, therefore, becomes a much broader concept, rooted in the quality of one's actions and the ability to remain consistent with one's core principles.

Vision and Values: The Life Project

Once the foundations are solid, you can begin to build the rest of your life and business. But the vision is only as strong as the values on which it is based. Values are the moral compass that guides every decision, every action, every relationship. Without values, it's like wanting to build a house without a plan. For me, the foundations of self-awareness, discipline, and purpose created the ground for a clear vision. Over time, I built a vision deeply rooted in my values: hard work, integrity, family, and growth. These values became my guiding principles. When I made decisions, I made them based on whether they aligned with my values. When I faced challenges, I reminded myself of these values. With a strong vision and clear values, everything else falls into place. Every step I took after this realization was an action aligned with my deepest beliefs, and that's when I started seeing results that truly mattered.

The Strength of the Present: Building a Solid Mind

"Success is built in the present, not in the past."

Being self-aware brings another layer of mindfulness—being present.

Imagine an experienced bricklayer at work, in front of a structure yet to be completed. He has a clear vision of the final result, but he knows that the beauty and strength of the building depend not only on the overall design but also on the care with which each individual brick is laid. In those moments, the bricklayer is fully present. He doesn't think about the future or the past; he is focused on placing that brick exactly in its place. This is a fundamental lesson for life and business. Too often, we let our minds wander, dwelling on past mistakes or future worries. But just as the bricklayer avoids thinking about the entire structure while placing each brick, we must train ourselves to stay in the present. Only by doing so can we build solid foundations that won't collapse under the weight of regret or fear.

The Trap of the Past and the Fear of Collapse: Live in the Present to Avoid It

The human mind tends to focus on past mistakes, replaying in a loop what we could have done differently. These regrets are like damaged bricks that, when used as a foundation, make every new construction fragile. Living in the past is like trying to build a future on uncertain ground because we waste mental and emotional energy thinking about what we cannot change. This attitude not only immobilizes us but also prevents us from moving forward, as we remain anchored to what has been, rather than focusing on the present and the future we can build. Similarly, the fear of failure, the anxiety about what might go wrong, is like an impending collapse that undermines the strength of every action. Like a distracted bricklayer who doesn't carefully place the brick, every unhandled fear and concern compromises our ability to build a solid foundation. If we allow ourselves to be overwhelmed by the fear of collapse, we risk building on fragile foundations, weakening the entire structure of our lives. Self-awareness allows us to recognize these patterns, stop, and understand how our past, along with the fear of the future, influences our mental state and our ability to act in the present. The key to avoiding this psychological collapse is the ability to inhabit the present moment. Staying in the present means not allowing the past to dictate our actions and not letting the fear of failure paralyze us. It is only through self-awareness that we can reduce the impact of past regrets and future fears, creating a solid mental foundation free of anxiety. This approach allows us to face every new challenge with clarity and determination, without being overwhelmed by what we cannot control. In building our lives, just like in a construction project, every decision, every step, must be made with awareness and attention. We cannot afford to act impulsively or worriedly, but we must work with the confidence that every "brick" we lay on our path is done with awareness, free from regrets of the past and fears for the future. Only then can we build a solid future, resilient to obstacles, and capable of bearing the weight of challenges that will inevitably come.

The Mind as a Bricklayer: Building Strong Mental Foundations

The quality of your thoughts determines the strength of your mind. If you allow your mind to slip into negativity, worry, or doubt, it's like using faulty bricks in your mental construction.On the other hand, by staying present—aware of your thoughts and intentionally choosing positive and constructive thoughts—you begin to build a strong and resilient mind. This solid mental foundation will allow you to face challenges, obstacles, and failures without collapsing. When you are in the present, your mind becomes a tool at your service. It is not distracted by fears, anxieties, or regrets. It is a tool that helps you create. By staying present, you shift your mental energy from the fear of making mistakes to focusing on action. Every thought, like every brick, contributes to building your inner structure.

Conclusion: The Key to Lasting Success

Self-awareness is the foundation on which every great success is built, both in life and in business. Without a solid understanding of ourselves, our motivations, and our goals, challenges become insurmountable obstacles, and every success risks being unstable. Only with a clear vision of who we are and what we truly want can we face the future with determination and consistency. Self-awareness is not a destination but an ongoing journey, a process that requires commitment, reflection, and courage. It is what allows us to build not only a solid business but also a life rich in meaning and aligned with our values. With discipline and a clear purpose, we can face every difficulty and continue to grow, making each step an opportunity to build something that will withstand the test of time.

12

The Power of Self-Discipline

"Self-discipline is the bridge between goals and success." Jim Rohn

Self-discipline is one of the most powerful and decisive forces on the path to success. It is the engine that drives focus and determination, allowing us to overcome obstacles, stay focused on long-term goals, and ultimately achieve extraordinary results. In a world full of personal and professional challenges, self-discipline becomes the solid foundation on which to build a successful career and a fulfilling life. Without it, even the brightest talent risks remaining just untapped potential.

In my journey, discipline has been one of the key elements that allowed me to navigate the entrepreneurial path successfully. Having never had a real experience as an employee, the discipline I developed in the construction sector and in the business world has been fundamental to my approach. It wasn't a force imposed by someone else, but the awareness that, to grow a project, every small action had to be built with care and continuity, just like I would in a construction site.

Motivation vs. Self-Discipline

We often hear about motivation as the force that drives us to act, but it's essential to understand the difference between motivation and self-discipline. Motivation is the spark that ignites suddenly, fueling enthusiasm and the desire to take action. It is the initial thrill we feel when we have an idea, a project, or a goal that excites us. However, motivation is unstable: it can be strong today but fade tomorrow, influenced by emotions, difficulties, or unforeseen events.

Self-discipline, on the other hand, is the force that pushes us to keep working even when motivation fades. It is the ability to act regardless of our mood, the difficulties we face, or the temptations that distract us.

I never had the security of a stable job, only the drive of a clear vision. It was self-discipline that allowed me to work even when motivation wavered, facing challenges and staying focused on my goals.

The Motivation Trap

Many people believe that motivation must be present before starting any important task. In other words, they think they need to feel "inspired" or enthusiastic before acting. But in reality, motivation can be elusive. It may seem like there's never enough energy or desire to begin a project, especially if it's something difficult or challenging. However, what is often discovered is that motivation doesn't appear out of nowhere. Instead, motivation comes from the action itself. When you take the first step, even if you don't feel "ready," your brain begins to recognize progress and movement, which pushes you to continue. It's not so much motivation that creates action, but action that generates motivation. The true secret to overcoming this trap is to start without expecting to feel motivated right away and by using self-discipline let the energy come as you move forward.

Don't Seek Emotional Peaks

Many people are drawn to the idea of experiencing constant emotional highs–those moments of great motivation when you feel invincible. But this is unrealistic. Motivation is not a rollercoaster of emotional highs and lows. When you focus only on these emotional peaks, you risk becoming disappointed when motivation dips. A healthier approach is to let go of the idea that motivation should be an intense and constant emotional experience. Instead, the more useful attitude is to build a consistent and pragmatic mindset. Success is not made up of moments of exhilaration, but of regular and methodical activity. Don't seek the emotional peak that drives you to begin, but rather embrace the reality that success is built through calm and continuous progression.

Construction as a Metaphor for Discipline

Discipline is like building a house: it requires a clear vision of the project then patience and constant effort. The quality of the foundation will determine the strength of the final result, and this is where discipline plays the main role: building step by step, never neglecting the details, even when the final result is not yet visible.

At first, you might not see the immediate result of your effort, but every small step brings you closer to building something great. Self-discipline is the hand that holds the trowel, aligning every brick precisely.

In the world of construction, discipline is also related to the ability to follow regulations and rules. Just like a construction site must adhere to precise safety measures and building codes, our entrepreneurial journey needs to be structured and controlled. Every decision, every step, must be made with a clear mind, like a builder following the guidelines of a well-designed project. Without discipline, the risk of deviating from the rules is high, and the project can collapse like a building built without the proper foundations.

Focus as the Grounds of Success

In an increasingly hectic world, where distractions seem to be everywhere, maintaining focus becomes the main challenge to face. The temptations to deviate from the established path are numerous. However, it is self-discipline that provides us with the inner strength to stay on the right track. It's not enough to have a brilliant start; the true test comes when, over the long term, it is necessary to remain consistent and persistent, day after day.

In my path, there have been moments when the temptation to abandon everything and take a step back was strong. When obstacles seemed insurmountable or results didn't come immediately, it was my self-discipline that allowed me to keep going. Every step, even the smallest, contributed to building a vision that, though still under construction, was becoming clearer and clearer. The ability to persevere, to continue working even when motivation faltered, is what made my success possible.

Techniques for Developing Self-Discipline

Self-discipline is not an innate gift, but a skill that develops over time. Its strength grows with constant practice and the awareness that every small daily effort is a step toward success. In this chapter, I want to share with you some of the techniques I've applied in my journey to strengthen my self-discipline and stay focused on my long-term goals.

Focus on Small Progress

A common mistake is thinking that only big successes are worth noting. Many people are so focused on the end result that they overlook the small daily progress. However, it's precisely this attention to small steps that can generate the motivation needed to keep going. When you make even the slightest progress, even if it's not immediately visible globally, your brain recognizes it as a positive result. Every small success builds confidence and enthusiasm for the next step. Don't expect progress to always be spectacular; the true success lies in accumulating small victories every day. Additionally, these small daily accomplishments give you the momentum to tackle bigger challenges. Every step you take brings you closer to your goal, and seeing progress, even if minimal, can be one of the strongest sources of motivation.

Define Clear and Achievable Goals

A goal without clarity is not a goal it's just a wish. To build anything worthwhile, whether a skyscraper or a successful life, you need a vision so precise it feels like you can touch it. Every goal must be well-defined, measurable, and aligned with your long-term vision, just like a builder's blueprint that maps out every beam and bolt before construction begins. But clarity alone isn't enough. To make your goals achievable, you must break them down into smaller, manageable sub-goals. Think of them as the individual bricks that form the foundation of your dream. Consider a contractor tasked with building a bridge. They don't simply say, "I want a bridge." They define exactly what they need: a 500-meter suspension bridge, completed in two years, capable of supporting 10,000 vehicles daily. They set milestones securing materials by month three, completing the foundation by month nine, and measure progress at every step. This precision keeps the project on track, fuels motivation, and allows them to pivot when challenges arise, like delays or budget constraints. In the same way, your goals need this level of detail. Instead of saying, "I want to be successful," define what success looks like: "I want to launch a business that generates $100,000 in revenue within two years." Then, break it down: research the market in one month, draft a business plan in three months, secure funding by month six. To put this into action, take a moment to write down one goal that aligns with your long-term vision. Make it specific: What do you want to achieve? By when? How will you measure success? Then, list three sub-goals that will move you closer to it. This blueprint will not only keep you motivated but also empower you to build your future, one deliberate step at a time. As I often say, "A builder doesn't dream of walls he plans every brick."

Establish Routines and Habits

The idea that motivation must be present every time you face a task is a dangerous myth. In fact, motivation is unpredictable and fluctuating. Sometimes you wake up with incredible energy, ready to tackle the day, but other times it's hard to even get out of bed. The solution to this uncertainty is creating routines and habits. Habits don't depend on the emotions of the moment, but are actions you perform automatically without having to think each time about whether you're motivated or not. If you create a routine that allows you to work regularly and systematically, motivation becomes less important. The consistent repetition of activities and goals gives you a sense of progress, which, over time, strengthens your intrinsic motivation. Having established habits allows you to move forward even on days when you're less motivated because the action is already scheduled.

Apply the Two-Minute Rule

Procrastination is often one of the biggest obstacles to productivity. The longer we delay tasks, the more they accumulate and the more overwhelming they can become. A strategy that has proven incredibly effective for me in overcoming procrastination is the two-minute rule. This simple yet powerful technique is designed to tackle small tasks immediately before they can become distractions.

The two-minute rule is based on the idea that if a task will take two minutes or less to complete, there's no reason to put it off. Instead of saving it for later, you handle it right away. Whether it's replying to an email, making a quick phone call, tidying up a small area, or jotting down a note, these tasks can be completed almost effortlessly in a very short period. The beauty of this approach is that it creates a rapid momentum and helps keep your workflow uninterrupted.

Build Mental Resilience

Self-discipline alone is not enough to guarantee success; it must be paired with mental resilience. This is the ability to stay strong, adaptable, and focused in the face of adversity. As an entrepreneur, you will inevitably encounter challenges, like financial struggles, unexpected market shifts, team conflicts, or personal difficulties. They are an unavoidable part of the journey. Resilience is what allows you to persist through these tough moments. The more resilient you become, the more disciplined you will be, and the more disciplined you are, the stronger your resilience will grow.

Resilience is the mental muscle that keeps you from succumbing to discouragement or burnout. It's the internal strength that enables you to continue working towards your goals, even when faced with failure, disappointment, or exhaustion. Doubt or frustration will always arise, but responding to these emotions with resilience allows you to acknowledge setbacks and difficult emotions without letting them derail your progress.

Don't Neglect Self-Care

Self-discipline is often mistakenly viewed as a rigid, single-minded focus on work and achievement. Many people associate discipline with grinding through long hours, sacrificing their personal needs in the pursuit of success. However, true self-discipline is not about pushing yourself to the point of exhaustion; it is about creating a balance that nurtures both your ambition and your well-being. Neglecting self-care is one of the most common and harmful mistakes that driven entrepreneurs make. In the long term, neglecting your body and mind can significantly hinder your performance and undermine your ability to achieve your goals. See chapter 8 for the importance of self-care.

Learn to Delay Gratification

One of the most powerful traits of self-discipline is the ability to delay gratification. In a world where instant results and rewards are often just a click away, learning to resist the temptation of immediate pleasure can be one of the most challenging yet transformative skills to develop. However, it is a critical component of success, particularly when it comes to building a career or a business.

The more you practice delaying gratification, the more you realize that the journey itself, with its challenges and setbacks, is often more fulfilling than the instant pleasures that distract you from your ultimate goals. This practice builds resilience, focus, and an unwavering commitment to your vision. It is an acknowledgment that the best rewards come not from fleeting moments of pleasure but from sustained effort, consistency, and perseverance over time.

Conclusion

Self-discipline is the cornerstone of success all aspects of life. It is not merely a matter of willpower, but of consistent, purposeful action, even when motivation fades. True acheivement does not come from the fleeting bursts of motivation, but from the steady, disciplined work that we put in, day after day. It's about making small, continuous improvements and knowing that each moment of focus brings us closer to our ultimate goal.

Ultimately, self-discipline is not just about achieving success; it's about creating a mindset that allows us to rise above obstacles, maintain clarity of purpose, and build a life and career grounded in focus, determination, and resilience. As I've discovered throughout my journey, building a strong foundation of self-discipline allows us to weather challenges and stay focused on long-term goals. In the end, the results speak for themselves: success is built one disciplined step at a time.

13

The Power of Persistence

"Success is not final, failure is not fatal: it is the courage to continue that counts." Winston Churchill

In life and business, obstacles are inevitable. But how we respond to these obstacles is what determines whether we will succeed or fail. Persistent determination is the force that drives us forward when circumstances seem to be against us. It is the resilience to keep pushing toward our goals despite the obstacles, failures, and delays that inevitably arise along the way.

The lessons learned through perseverance are invaluable, not only for achieving success but also for cultivating personal growth and adaptability.

The Essence of Persistence: Overcoming Obstacles

Persistent determination is the ability to keep going despite adversity. In my life, there have been countless moments where I faced obstacles that seemed insurmountable, times when everything seemed to go wrong. Yet, every time, perseverance allowed me to move forward.

One of the hardest lessons to learn was that failure is not the opposite of success, but part of success. The path to achieving goals is rarely linear and often includes moments of doubt, confusion, and failure. It is precisely in those moments that persistent determination is put to the test.

Persistence vs. Stubbornness: Knowing the Difference

It's important to distinguish between perseverance and stubbornness. Perseverance involves flexibility, adaptation, and learning from failures, while stubbornness is the opposite, often involving a refusal to change or accept new ways of thinking when something isn't working. Perseverance is not about continuing down a path that leads to nowhere; it's about reassessing, adapting, and moving forward with renewed purpose.

For instance, there were times in my journey when I was so determined to make a particular business model work that I almost ignored the signs it was failing. I had to realize that true perseverance is knowing when it's time to change direction and adjust course, not just blindly continuing without evaluation. Perseverance means being unwavering in the pursuit of your goals, but also having the wisdom to modify your approach when necessary.

How to Cultivate Persistence

Embrace Failure as a Teacher: Failure doesn't define you, it refines you. Every failure brings with it valuable lessons that can propel you toward your next success. Understanding that failure is simply a part of the process can lessen its sting and help you move forward with resilience. The more we embrace failure as a lesson rather than a defeat, the stronger our persistence becomes.

Break Goals into Manageable Steps: Persistence is not just about aiming for one overwhelming big goal. It's about making constant progress, step by step. Breaking larger goals into smaller, more manageable tasks can prevent burnout and provide continuous forward momentum. Celebrate every small victory along the way and let it propel you toward the next challenge.

Maintain a Growth Mindset: Persistence thrives in an environment where growth is a priority. A growth mindset–believing that we can improve through effort and learning–is essential for maintaining persistence over the long term. When facing challenges, people with a growth mindset look for solutions and ways to improve, rather than seeing obstacles as insurmountable walls.

Create a Support Network: While persistence often requires solo effort, you don't have to do it alone. Surround yourself with people who encourage, inspire, and challenge you. The support of others can help you stay grounded and motivated. A mentor, trusted colleague, or even family and friends can offer valuable perspectives that help you overcome tough times.

Stay Focused on Your "Why": In moments of doubt, reconnecting with your "why" can fuel your persistence. Why are you pursuing your goals? What drives you forward? Keeping your sense of purpose clear in your mind can be the fuel you need to keep going, even when the path seems uncertain or difficult.

Practice Patience: Persistence requires patience. It's easy to want immediate results, but success doesn't come overnight. In business, as in life, things take time. Understanding that persistence is about the long game, not the quick win, helps you maintain the strength to keep going, even when progress seems slow.

The Rewards of Persistence

While persistence is often a challenging journey, the rewards are immeasurable. The ability to weather storms, face challenges, and keep moving forward despite uncertainty leads to success that is earned, not given. The power of persistence is evident not only in achieving your goals, but in the person you become along the way.

One of the most gratifying things about persistence is the sense of pride and accomplishment that comes from achieving something that once seemed impossible. It's the deep satisfaction of knowing that, no matter how many times you've been knocked down, you found the strength to get back up and keep going.

Conclusion: The Unbreakable Forge of Persistence

Persistence isn't just a trait, it's the fire that tempers the steel of your soul, the hammer that shapes the raw iron of your dreams into something unyielding. In the vast worksite of life and business, where storms rage and obstacles trip you up, it's not the absence of struggle that defines success, but the courage to grip your tools tighter and keep building. This is the power of persistence; it doesn't crack under doubt, but rises stronger with every blow.

Persistence isn't blind stubbornness. It's the wisdom to shift your stance and strike again with purpose.

PART THREE

PRACTICAL TOOLS: BUILDING SUCCESS DAY BY DAY

14

The Master Plan: From Vision to Victory

"A goal without a plan is just a wish. Transform your vision into action, and watch your dreams take shape." Antoine de Saint-Exupéry

In construction, every successful project begins with a blueprint. It's the detailed plan, the roadmap that guides every step, ensuring that the final product is built to last. The same applies to life and business; without a clear blueprint, you are navigating blind. This chapter is designed to give you a clear, step-by-step guide to transform the principles from this book into tangible results in your life and business. Using the same strategic approach that architects apply to creating a building, we will break down the process into manageable steps, helping you create a concrete action plan with short-term and long-term goals, and equipping you with the tools needed to execute your vision.

Personal Story: The Power of Careful Planning and Strategy in Achieving Goals

From early on in my journey, planning played a crucial role in turning my ideas into reality. My experience in construction taught me the importance of thinking ahead. Every project I undertook required a detailed plan that included timelines, resources, budget allocation, and risk management. This roadmap was a clear vision of what the final structure will look like. Without this initial plan, the entire project risks becoming a chaotic, unmanageable mess.

The importance of planning became even clearer to me during a pivotal moment in my career. Early in my business journey, I took on a large project that, at the time, seemed like the breakthrough opportunity I needed. However, due to a lack of proper planning and unrealistic expectations, the project became an enormous headache. Deadlines were missed, costs were inflated, and clients were unhappy. It was a wake-up call. I realized that without a detailed plan, even the most promising opportunities could turn into disasters.

After this failure, I took a step back and re-evaluated everything. I applied the lessons I had learned from construction projects, breaking down the big tasks into smaller, achievable goals, setting clear deadlines, and planning for risks. The next time I took on a major project, I had a roadmap, contingency plans, and a solid team behind me. This careful planning not only helped me succeed in that project, but it also helped me build a reputation for reliability and excellence in the industry.

One of the key lessons I learned along the way is that planning is preparation, not prediction. By taking the time to plan, I put myself in the best possible position to handle whatever unforeseen circumstances came my way.

Once I put in a structured approach to my business, I saw real progress. The journey wasn't always easy, but having a clear vision and a strategic plan made all the difference. The power of planning lies in its ability to create structure and direction, ensuring that every effort is purposeful and aligned with the desired outcome. Planning didn't just help me succeed in business, it became a guiding principle for life.

Breaking Down Big Goals into Smaller, Actionable Steps

One of the biggest challenges in both business and life is tackling big, seemingly overwhelming goals. At the beginning, I often faced projects and ambitions that felt far beyond my capabilities. But over time, I learned the crucial lesson of breaking down large goals into manageable chunks, steps that could be executed one at a time.

Start by identifying the big picture: What do you want your life or business to look like in five or ten years? Once you have that vision, break it down into yearly, monthly, and even weekly goals. Then, turn those goals into daily actions that will move you closer to success.

For example, when I first started my building business, the idea of scaling it up seemed daunting. But I knew that I couldn't grow overnight. Instead, I broke the growth process into manageable phases: first securing a few clients, then hiring a small team, and gradually expanding my operations. By focusing on one step at a time, I was able to build momentum and turn my big goal into a reality.

This same strategy applies to personal goals as well. When I decided to become a better leader, I didn't just aim for broad success. I broke down the goal of improving my leadership skills into smaller, more specific actions, such as reading leadership books, attending seminars, practicing communication, and seeking mentorship. By continuously breaking down larger objectives into achievable actions, I was able to create lasting change in both my business and personal life.

A Roadmap for Success: Tools and Techniques for Effective Planning, Inspired by Construction Project Management

My years in the construction industry taught me valuable tools and techniques for planning and project management that are just as applicable in business. Construction projects require meticulous organization, constant monitoring, and the ability to adapt to changes. These same principles translated well into the way I planned and executed business objectives.

To make your blueprint as effective as possible, it's crucial to focus on the following elements:

Clarity: Your vision should be crystal clear. Don't just think about what you want, but be specific about how you want to get there. Ask yourself what success looks like to you.

Action: Set clear, actionable goals that will lead you to your vision. Each action should build on the previous one, propelling you toward your desired outcome.

Flexibility: Just as construction plans often need to be adjusted midway, your blueprint should remain flexible. Life and business are dynamic, and obstacles will inevitably arise. Adapt your plan as needed while staying true to your long-term vision.

Consistency: Consistency is the key to turning a blueprint into a tangible outcome. Small, daily actions compound over time and lead to big results.

Creating a Timeline: In construction, every project is given a strict timeline with deadlines broken into daily, weekly, and monthly milestones. This helps keep everything on track and ensures that progress is always measurable.

Risk Management: Construction projects involve countless risks, from weather disruptions to unforeseen expenses. By identifying risks early, I learned to factor these potential risks into my plans and create backup and mitigation strategies.

Resource Allocation: Just like a construction project requires resources, such as labor, materials, and equipment, business goals require resources as well. These might include time, money, talent, and energy. Avoid wasting these valuable resources by identifying which ones are necessary for your goals and ensure they are appropriately allocated.

Delegation and Teamwork: Construction is a team effort, and success is impossible without a great team. Whether it's skilled workers on a construction site or a dedicated business team, delegation is key to success. I learned to trust the strengths of others, assign roles, and foster a collaborative environment where everyone works towards the same goal.

Review and Adaptation: In construction, projects are constantly reviewed and adjusted to stay on track. This same approach is invaluable in business and life. I learned to assess progress regularly and make adjustments to ensure I was always moving forward.

Creating an Actionable Plan

An action plan is your roadmap for success. It takes the vision you've built and turns it into clear, actionable steps. Here's how to create one that will keep you focused and moving toward your goals.

1. **Start with Your Vision**

Begin by revisiting the vision for your life or business. What do you want to achieve in the long run? This is your guiding principle. Everything else in your action plan should support this overarching vision. Spend time refining this vision to ensure it's aligned with your values, and then break it down into smaller, more manageable pieces.

2. Set SMART Goals

Goals should be Specific, Measurable, Achievable, Relevant and Time-bound. Use the SMART framework to create goals that are clear and structured. For example:

- Specific: "I want to increase my business revenue by 20% this year."

- Measurable: "I will track progress monthly using financial reports."

- Achievable: "I will review my operations and identify at least three areas for improvement."

- Relevant: "This goal supports my vision of growing my business sustainably."

- Time-bound: "I aim to achieve this within the next 12 months."

3. Break Goals into Actionable Steps

Each goal should be broken down into smaller tasks. These tasks are the building blocks that will bring your goal to life. For instance, if your goal is to increase revenue, smaller tasks could include researching new marketing strategies, reaching out to potential clients, and refining your product offerings.

4. Create Short-Term Milestones

Short-term milestones are the checkpoints that keep you on track. These should be goals or targets that you can reach within 1 to 3 months. They give you a sense of progress and allow you to make adjustments before moving on to bigger objectives. For example:

"In 30 days, secure 3 new clients."

"In 60 days, implement a new digital marketing campaign."

"In 90 days, evaluate and optimize business operations."

5. Plan for Long-Term Success

Long-term goals are where you want to be in the next 1 to 5 years. These goals require a more strategic and sustained effort. Think about where you want your business or life to be at the end of this period. These might include launching new products, expanding into new markets, or reaching a specific level of financial freedom. Be sure to align these long-term goals with your vision and values.

Practical Worksheets and Templates

To ensure that you stay on track and organized, use the following worksheets and templates to facilitate your goal-setting and execution process. These tools will help you put theory into practice, stay focused, and measure your progress.

Vision Statement Worksheet

Clarify your vision for your life or business by answering the following questions:

What do I want to achieve in the long term?

How do I want to impact others or the world around me?

What core values will guide my decisions?

What legacy do I want to leave behind?

Goal-Setting Template

Use this template to write down your SMART goals, both short-term and long-term:

Goal Name:

Specific Goal:

Measurable Outcome:

Achievable Steps:

Relevant to My Vision:

Timeframe for Completion:

Action Steps Breakdown

Break down each goal into smaller tasks and prioritize them:

Goal:

Task 1: [Action Step]

Task 2: [Action Step]

Task 3: [Action Step]

[Continue as needed]

Deadline for Task Completion:

Weekly and Monthly Planning Templates

Organize your weeks and months to stay consistent with your goals:

Weekly Planning:

This Week's Focus:

Action Steps to Complete:

Deadline for Completion:

Monthly Planning:

This Month's Focus:

Action Steps to Complete:

Review Date: (Set a time to review progress and make adjustments)

Execution Tracker

Keep track of your daily progress:

Date:

Action Taken:

Progress Toward Goal:

Challenges Faced:

Next Steps:

Maintaining Momentum and Overcoming Setbacks

Creating an action plan is only the first step. Execution is where the magic happens. However, there will be challenges along the way. To maintain momentum:

Stay Consistent: Even when progress feels slow, consistency will pay off over time. Don't get discouraged by small setbacks.

Celebrate Milestones: Recognize and celebrate your wins, both big and small. This helps you stay motivated and reinforces the positive habits you're building.

Reassess Regularly: Every 3 to 6 months, revisit your goals and action plan. Are they still aligned with your vision? Do you need to adjust your strategies based on your progress and any new circumstances?

Conclusion: Building Your Blueprint for Success and Turning Vision into Reality

This chapter has been a call to action–a reminder that planning is not just a step in the process; it's the foundation of everything you hope to achieve. Success doesn't happen by accident. It's not a stroke of luck or a fleeting moment of inspiration, it's the result of careful planning, intentional action, and unwavering focus.

Every principle I've shared with you in this book isn't just theory. These are the same tools I have used in my career, which helped me overcome huge challenges, build successful businesses, and grow personally. The lessons I've learned from construction have shaped not only my business, but also my approach to life. They've taught me that success is not about hoping for the best; it's about preparing for it.

Just as a construction project begins with a blueprint, your life and business require a clear, actionable plan to guide you toward your goals. Without it, you're building on shaky ground, risking collapse when challenges arise.

But planning is more than just a practical tool; it's a mindset. It's taking control of your destiny, refusing to leave your future to chance, and committing to the daily actions that will move you closer to your vision. It's understanding that every great achievement, whether it's a towering skyscraper or a thriving business, starts with a single, well-thought-out blueprint.

So, as you move forward, I challenge you to take ownership of your journey. Define your vision with clarity. Break it down into actionable steps. Anticipate the challenges and prepare for them. And most importantly, stay consistent. Remember, the small, daily actions you take today will compound over time, creating the life and business you've always dreamed of.

Success is not a destination; it's a journey. And with a solid blueprint in hand, you'll be ready to navigate every twist and turn, every obstacle and opportunity, with confidence and purpose. Build your plan. Take the first step. And watch as your vision comes to life, one intentional action at a time.

The blueprint is yours to design. Now, go build something extraordinary.

15

Time Management

"Non est quod tempus non satis sit, sed quod multis non satis sit ad tempus regendum."

"It is not that we have a short time to live, but that we waste much of it." Seneca, *De Brevitate Vitae*

Time is one of the few resources that we cannot acquire more of. For this reason, mastering time management is crucial not only for success in business but also for personal well-being. Whether you are managing a business, balancing family life, or focusing on personal development, effective time management allows you to keep everything in order and avoid burnout.

Mastering the Art of Time Management

In my journey, especially during the early years of managing my businesses, time management was a constant challenge. The demands of construction projects, client meetings, and daily operations could have easily overwhelmed anyone. I quickly realized that without a structured approach to time management, I would not have been able to keep up with the workload and responsibilities.

To handle multiple responsibilities, I adopted a disciplined approach to planning. I knew that if I didn't take control of my time, my time would take control of me. It wasn't always easy. There were moments when I had too many tasks and not enough hours in the day, but over time, I developed strategies that allowed me to handle everything with more confidence and less stress.

The Power of Time-Blocking and Prioritization

One of the most effective strategies I adopted was time-blocking. This meant dedicating specific blocks of time to different tasks and focusing exclusively on those during the designated time. I divided my day into segments, often starting early with the most important tasks. For example, in the morning, I would tackle the most mentally demanding tasks, like strategic planning for my building business, Florence Homes. Then, I reserved blocks of time for client calls, project management, and check-ins with my teams. The Pomodoro technique is great for 30-minute focussed sessions.

Prioritization was equally crucial. There's always more to do than time allows. I learned to be relentless about determining which tasks truly required my attention and which could be delegated or postponed. I adopted the mindset that not everything on the to-do list is urgent, and I began identifying high-priority tasks–those that would have the greatest impact on business and personal goals. This allowed me to focus my energy on what truly mattered, instead of scattering myself too thin.

Delegation: The Key to Scaling

As my businesses grew, so did the number of responsibilities to manage. It was at this point that I truly understood the power of delegation. Delegating tasks became essential to maintaining efficiency while still focusing on high-level responsibilities like business development and leadership. I realized I didn't have to do everything myself, and that entrusting tasks to the right people allowed me to step back and focus on the bigger picture.

I worked closely with my project managers, assistants, and even subcontractors, empowering them to make decisions and take ownership of projects. Effective delegation freed me to concentrate on the vision, while others handled the details. This also helped build a culture of trust and accountability within my teams, where people felt motivated to take initiative and achieve results.

Tools and Strategies for Productive Time Management

Over the years, I refined my approach to time management with some additional tools and strategies. Here are a few that made a significant difference in both my professional and personal life:

Time Tracking Apps: I used time-tracking apps to get an overview of where my time was going. It's easy to get lost in emails or administrative tasks, but time tracking made me more aware of how I was spending my day. This helped eliminate time-wasters and adjust my schedule accordingly.

Setting Clear Goals: At the start of each week, I set clear, measurable goals for myself. These goals became the framework for my time-blocking planning. If a task didn't contribute to the weekly objectives, I re-evaluated its importance.

Review and Adjustments: Every day, I took a few minutes to review my time management. Did I stick to my schedule? Were there tasks I could have done more efficiently? This reflection helped me fine-tune my approach and continuously improve my time management system.

Saying No: One of the most important lessons I've learned in time management is that saying "no" is a crucial part of the process. Early on, I was eager to seize every opportunity, but over time, I realized that not every opportunity aligned with my vision or values. Learning to say "no" freed up time to focus on what truly mattered.

Work-Life Integration: Beyond Balance

Time management is often seen as an act of balancing work and life, but I believe in the concept of work-life integration. Balance suggests that work and personal life are separate entities, while integration recognizes that they are interconnected, and true harmony comes from making both work together to serve your overall goals.

For me, integrating time with family, personal development, and business has been crucial. For example, I used my time at the gym to listen to business podcasts, transforming it into a productive part of my day. Similarly, I made sure to include moments of rest and relaxation in my time-blocking schedule to recharge. Over time, I learned that time management is not just about doing more, but creating a life that is both productive and fulfilling.

Conclusion

Time management is a skill that is constantly evolving. What works today may need adjustments tomorrow. But with time-blocking, prioritization, and effective delegation, we can ensure that we're not just working more, but working smarter. The more we master the art of time management, the more we can focus on our true goals and create space for what matters most, both in business and in life.

Time is our most precious asset. How we use it defines our success, our relationships, and our well-being. Mastering it isn't just about efficiency, it's about making every moment count, so that when we look back, we know we spent our time on what truly mattered.

16

Tools of Tomorrow: Innovation for Success

"We don't just use technology, we live technology." Godfrey Reggio

In a world that never stands still, innovation means survival. From the leather-scented air of my grandfather's workshop to the hum of algorithms in today's construction sites, I've learned that innovation and efficiency are two sides of the same coin. Without using the new tools at our disposal, our productivity will tank. In today's fast-paced world, success is working smarter, not harder. The strategic use of the right tools, systems, and technologies will amplify your efforts. This chapter explores the importance of selecting the right tools and how to leverage them effectively to streamline your path to success.

From Saddles to AI: A Journey of Innovation

My story begins in the rugged hills of Sardinia, watching my grandfather stitch saddles day in, day out. He didn't know computers, but he knew evolution as he crafted equipment for a world that moved on horseback. Fast forward to the 1990s, and the internet roared into the world, turning blueprints into bytes and cracking open new ways to measure, plan, and connect. And now, we welcome AI, a tool so sharp it cuts through the impossible, transforming data into decisions faster than I could swing a hammer. Innovation isn't reserved for tech giants; it's the grit in your hands, the will to ask, "How can I make this better?"

Innovation is survival. It's a mindset that sees challenges as opportunities, not dead ends. It's asking, "What can I do differently?" instead of "This doesn't work." It's the courage to abandon the old when the new beckons, as I did when I traded my grandfather's needle for the web's endless threads, then embraced AI to reforge my craft. But innovation alone is a half-built house. Efficiency is the mortar that binds it, turning vision into action with precision and power.

The Importance of Innovation in Life and Business

Innovation isn't a sideline, it's the heartbeat of progress, the pulse that keeps both life and business alive in an environment of change. I've stood on muddy ground, watching competitors wield tools I didn't grasp, and realized that without innovation, I wasn't just behind; I was buried. It's the difference between surviving a season and dominating an era. Companies like Tesla don't thrive by resting on old engines; they roar ahead by reimagining what an engine can be. Innovation isn't optional, it's the oxygen of growth.

In life, it's no less vital. When I first synced my days with a digital calendar, it wasn't just time saved; I gained clarity, a life unshackled from chaos. Innovation lifts us beyond the grind. Health apps whisper warnings before illness strikes, virtual tutors craft minds, and AI assistants weave order from the fray. It's personal evolution, a refusal to let the world outpace your spirit. My grandfather didn't stop at one saddle design; he quietly refined, adapted, and lived innovation. In life and business, it's the same: to stagnate is to fade, but to innovate is to reign.

Technology as the Engine of Efficiency

We don't just use technology; we live it. AI isn't the future; it's the present, accelerating change by automating the mundane and amplifying the brilliant. In construction, technology transformed my world. Cameras and sensors catch risks before they strike, sending real-time alerts to keep my crew safe; predictive maintenance spots machine failures before they halt a project; communication syncs designers, laborers and clients, like a well-oiled machine. Beyond the site, it's reshaped my life—Siri and Google Assistant organize my days, health apps track vitality, and virtual tutors personalize learning. This isn't ease; it's emancipation, freeing us to conquer bigger challenges.

The Power of Books: Learning from the Past

No success toolkit is complete without learning from the wisdom of others, and books are one of the most powerful tools for this. Books give you access to the experiences of successful individuals, offering lessons and insights that you can apply directly to your own life and business.

Books act as a mentor when you don't have one in person. They provide wisdom from the past, allowing you to learn from the mistakes and successes of others. This shortcut to learning helps you avoid common pitfalls and accelerates your growth. Every book is an opportunity to gain a new perspective, challenge your assumptions, and refine your strategies.

For me, books and magazines have had a huge impact on my personal growth and entrepreneurial journey. I realized in the early 90s that I needed to think differently, so I read and read. Those books and articles opened my eyes to the importance of mindset and habits in achieving success.

Since then, I've never stopped reading. Some of those books I've read at least 100 times, and I always return to them. Every time, I discover deeper meanings and new lessons.

Learning from the stories of others allows you to accelerate your success by leveraging their wisdom without having to face the same struggles. Books provide a chance to sit with great minds of the past and present and learn from their journey. They offer lessons on leadership, resilience, and strategy, all of which are critical for anyone striving to create something significant in life. Through books, you can learn to approach challenges with a mindset focused on growth rather than fear of failure.

The Power of Technology, Systems, and Learning

We are in a technological age with systems and tools that allow us to automate repetitive tasks, stay organized, track progress, and ultimately make better decisions faster. But the true power lies in using the right tools tailored to our unique needs. They can act as force multipliers, allowing us to get more done with less effort.

Best Practices for Implementing Tools

Once you've selected the right tools, it's crucial to implement them effectively. The real power of tools is unlocked when you integrate them into your workflow in a way that maximizes their impact. Here are some best practices for getting the most out of your tools:

1. Choose Tools That Integrate Well

The first step in leveraging technology effectively is to choose tools that work well together. When your tools integrate, you reduce manual data entry, eliminate redundancies, and streamline your workflow. For example, integrating your project management software with your communication platform or calendar helps ensure that everything works in harmony, making your day more productive and less stressful. Some examples include:

Google Calendar + Asana: Integrate Google Calendar with Asana to sync project deadlines with appointments, ensuring you never miss a deadline.

Zapier: Use Zapier to automate integration between various tools (e.g., Google Sheets, Trello, Gmail) to reduce the need for manual data entry.

2. Invest Time in Learning

The more you understand how to use your tools, the better you can leverage them. Take time to explore each tool's features and capabilities. By mastering the tools you use, you'll be able to streamline your processes and make better decisions. This investment in learning pays off by saving you time and effort in the long run.

3. Maintain Organization and Structure

Organization is key to efficiency. Keeping your tools well-organized ensures that you can easily access the information you need and helps keep your work environment free from clutter. Whether it's setting up clear folders, labeling files, or using templates, staying organized will make your entire workflow smoother and more efficient.

LinkedIn Learning: Offers courses on how to use specific software tools (e.g., Excel, Trello, Salesforce) to improve your competency in managing them.

YouTube: Use video tutorials to learn new features and tricks of the tools you use, such as those for Excel, Google Analytics, or marketing automation platforms.

Udemy: Purchase specific courses for the best use of professional software you employ in your workflow, such as business management software, CRMs, and design tools.

4. Regularly Review and Refine

Technology is constantly evolving, and so should your systems. Periodically review your tools and processes to ensure they are still aligned with your goals. Keep an eye out for new tools that could further optimize your workflow and be open to refining or changing your systems as necessary. Regular updates keep your tools fresh, relevant, and effective.

Conclusion: Streamlining Your Path to Success

Success is not just about working hard; it's about working smarter. The right tools, systems, and technology can help simplify processes, make better decisions, and achieve your goals more efficiently.

Just like in construction, where we've moved from using a water level to advanced electronic tools, from wooden measuring rods to laser meters, from hammers and chisels to sophisticated technologies, the evolution of tools is crucial in the pursuit of success. Every technological change improves precision, saves time, and optimizes efficiency, paving the way for possibilities that once seemed unimaginable.

Integrating the right tools into your daily operations gives you the freedom to focus on what matters most for your growth and legacy. By harnessing the power of books and technology, you can shorten your path to success, maximize your efforts, and move forward with confidence.

My grandfather's hands taught me to craft; the internet taught me to connect; AI taught me to soar. As you work to optimize your journey to success, remember that every tool you choose, every book you read, and every system you implement is an investment in your future. Choose wisely, keep learning, and execute with determination: soon, you'll see your dreams come to life.

17

Attention to Detail

"Success is the sum of small efforts, repeated day in and day out."
  Robert Collier

In construction, business, or any endeavor worth pursuing, significant results are not born from grand gestures, they emerge from the mastery of small details. If a joint, measurement, or even a stitch is overlooked, the entire structure falters. I've witnessed it, lived it, and learned it through hard-earned experience. This chapter is your technical guide to precision–straight from the field, no fluff, no shortcuts.

A Lesson in Leather

If you want a building that endures, the height is irrelevant. It's the foundation, the rebar, the mix that matters. The same principle applies to life: success isn't defined by a flashy finish but by the steady accumulation of small, deliberate actions. I learned this lesson early, watching my grandfather in his Sardinian workshop.

He wasn't just an old craftsman tinkering with leather; he was a master saddlemaker, creating pieces of lasting value, one stitch at a time.

I'll never forget those hours spent watching my grandfather at work. I'd sit there, mesmerized, as he shaped saddles with an almost surgical precision. He'd sit at his bench, tools laid out like a surgeon's instruments; knife sharp, awl steady, thread strong. I'd watch him pierce the leather, pull the stitch, check the tension over and over, each one identical to the last. He took his time over every cut of the hide, every pull of the needle, every knot, never skipping a step. His work was a testament to patience and care. Each stitch was tight, even, flawless.

His focus was absolute; nothing could break his concentration. He didn't speak much, but his actions spoke volumes: those details weren't trivial, they were the essence of his craft. A saddle took days, sometimes weeks, to complete, but when he finished, it wasn't just functional, it was a legacy.

Fifty years later, people still notice when I ride that saddle he made for me, still solid, still admired. That's the reward of attention to detail: it endures. I was just a kid back then, but I understood the difference. He didn't craft for the moment, but for decades ahead. Every stitch was a decision: do it right or don't do it at all. That saddle is still mine, still in use, still a testament to the power of precision. It's not just a piece of leather, it's a symbol of pride, strength, and work that stands the test of time.

That's what attention to detail delivers: it transforms the decent into the exceptional, the short-term into the timeless. In construction, a loose joint leaks. In business, a sloppy email erodes trust. In life, a missed detail can derail progress. Small efforts, consistently applied, build monumental outcomes. Overlook them, and you're setting yourself up for failure.

I've carried that lesson into my own work and life. On every construction site, every nail, every cut, every measurement must hold up like his stitches. And in my personal life, every decision, every interaction, every habit must be approached with the same care. Anything less is unacceptable.

Precision Isn't Perfection – It's Quality

Let's be clear: precision isn't chasing an unattainable ideal of perfection. It's caring enough to do things right. My grandfather didn't stitch those saddles to impress anyone. He did it because that's how you create something of value. Every action mattered: measure the hide twice, cut once, thread the needle cleanly, pull the stitch firmly. No waste, no shortcuts. That's the hallmark of quality–work that stands up under pressure and endures over time.

In my trade, I've built homes, offices, and legacies. The same principle applies. A wall is only as good as your level. A bid is only as solid as your numbers. One weak seam, one miscalculation, and the entire project is compromised. I've seen builders rush a foundation. It looks fine until the first rain, and then it's a disaster. Details are the backbone of any structure, physical or metaphorical. Skip them, and you're not just being careless, you're setting the stage for a failure that will cost far more to fix than it would have to prevent. Precision is your safeguard. Invest in it now, or pay the price later.

Building a Life, One Detail at a Time

The same principles that apply to construction and craftsmanship also apply to building a life. Your life is your most important project, and the details are what define its quality. Every decision, no matter how small, contributes to the overall structure. A missed opportunity, a neglected relationship, a hasty choice are the loose joints and weak seams that can compromise the integrity of your life.

Think of your daily habits as the stitches in a saddle. Each one may seem insignificant, but together they create something that can withstand the test of time. My grandfather's saddles didn't become legendary because of one perfect stitch. They endured because every stitch was perfect. Similarly, a life well-lived isn't the result of one grand achievement but the accumulation of small, consistent efforts.

For example, showing up on time, keeping your word, or taking a moment to listen to someone are the details that build trust, respect, and lasting relationships. In my own life, I've learned that dramatic gestures don't always ensure success, but the quiet, steady work of getting the little things right never fails. Whether, Small actions, like double-checking a measurement on site or taking the time to mentor a young worker, add up to something meaningful.

Operational Tactics: Wiring Precision Into Your Work and Life

Precision is a discipline you cultivate. Here's how I've learned to execute it, straight from the field:

1. Focus on the Process: Don't get lost in the end goal–master each step along the way. My grandfather didn't see a saddle; he saw the next stitch. On my sites, I don't see a house; I see the plumb line, the mortar, the block. In life, I don't see success; I see the daily habits, the small choices, the moments of integrity.

2. Break It Down: Large tasks can be overwhelming–break them into manageable parts. A saddle isn't one job; it's fifty stitches, ten cuts, five knots. A building isn't a single structure; it's a foundation, a frame, a roof. A life isn't one grand achievement; it's a series of small, consistent efforts.

3. Use Checklists: Systems are more reliable than memory. My grandfather had his tools in perfect order, every step ingrained. I rely on written checklists for every job: measure, cut, check, adjust. In life, I use goals and routines to keep myself on track.

4. Review Twice: Speed often sacrifices quality. My grandfather would test every stitch. If it was too loose, he'd redo it. I walk every site, check every line. If

something's off by a fraction, it gets fixed. In life, I take time to reflect on my actions and decisions, ensuring they align with my values.

5. Stay Present: Distractions are the enemy of precision. My grandfather would block out everything–no chatter, no interruptions. I do the same. One task, one move at a time. Multitasking leads to mistakes, whether on the job or in life.

Conclusion: Build It Right or Build It Again

Success isn't a matter of luck; it's the result of small things done well, day after day. My grandfather taught me that, stitch by stitch, in a quiet workshop. Every cut, every measurement, every pull of the needle built something that outlasted him, something I still use today.

That's the deal: precision is your tool, detail is your strength. You don't get there by guessing but by locking in, checking twice, and doing it right, even when no one's watching.

In this trade, you're only as good as your last job and your last job is only as good as the details you didn't skip. Rush it, and you'll be rebuilding next year. Get it right, and you'll leave behind work that stands strong for fifty years. That's not just a job, that's your legacy. Build it solid, or don't bother starting.

18

Execution is Key

"Ideas are the foundation, but execution is the structure that turns them into reality. Without action, dreams remain blueprints."
Mr. Ibba

When I think of an idea being properly realized, I imagine a well-designed construction. Every brick, every beam, every pillar must be placed correctly. The same thing happens when you realize a dream, a goal, or a vision. Every step must be executed with care to achieve a successful outcome. But success is never guaranteed by ideas alone. It is the action behind those ideas that ultimately determines whether they will come to life or remain just a thought. Execution is the key to turning dreams into reality, and without it, even the best plans are meaningless. In construction, a blueprint without execution is just paper and ink. In life, the same holds true for your goals and aspirations. But execution isn't always about precision or perfection. Sometimes, it's about the raw, unpolished action that gets you started, the gritty determination to take that first step, even when the path ahead is unclear. That's what I call 'raw action'. It's the kind of bold, unrefined effort that breaks through barriers and sets the stage for success.

The Critical Nature of Execution and Raw Action

Execution is the bridge that turns plans into reality. In construction, the most carefully drawn plans would be pointless without the work, resources, and energy to make them come to life. The same goes for your dreams.

I learned this lesson early in my career, during one of the most challenging periods of my life. After my divorce, I was starting from zero, with limited resources and a struggling business. I had just lost a major contract due to a competitor undercutting my bid, and I was on the verge of giving up. But I knew that if I didn't act, I'd lose everything I had worked for. So, I took a raw, uncalculated step. I drove to a nearby town, knocked on doors, and offered my services to anyone who would listen. It wasn't glamorous; I didn't have a polished pitch or a detailed plan. I was just a man with a hammer, a truck, and a desperate need to keep going. That raw action led to a small repair job for a local shopkeeper, which gave me the cash flow I needed to keep my crew paid and my business alive. It wasn't perfect, but it was the spark that got me moving again.

The danger of inaction, however, is that it creates a loop that's hard to escape. The longer we stay still, the more doubt, uncertainty, and hesitation take over, making the obstacles seem insurmountable. This cycle can become a downward spiral, feeding feelings of stagnation and despair–a loop that's difficult to break out of. But action, no matter how small, disrupts this cycle. Movement clears the mind, helps you think more clearly, and restores a sense of control. It's not about waiting for the perfect plan; it's about trusting that action itself will guide the way.

Raw action is the fuel that ignites execution, but it must be followed by careful execution to turn that initial spark into a lasting flame. The project may be perfect on paper, but if it is not executed with precision and care, the results will be far from desired. The quality of execution makes the difference between a job well done and one that could be dangerous or even fail. It is not the lack of ideas or projects that will cause a project to fail, but the negligence and superficiality with which they are implemented.

A Practical Example of What Happens When Execution Fails

A project that I personally followed comes to mind, relating to a Campidanese house of around 300 years old in the heart of Sardinia. The house, built of stone and mud and straw bricks, known as Ladiri in Sardinian, represented a piece of history and architectural tradition. The project had initially been entrusted to another company, but after an inspection by the engineers, they realized that the execution did not respect the plans, with serious risks for the stability of the building. The beams were undersized to support the weight of the stone walls, and the choice of materials was wrong for the type of work to be done. This raised concerns about the safety of the construction site and the resistance of the structure over time.

The company in charge of the project had not followed the plans. Not only had inadequate materials been chosen, but the beams were also insufficient for the heavy loads of the stone walls, compromising the safety of the structure. After taking charge of the project, we had to completely review the structural calculations, replace the beams with adequate dimensions and use the right materials to keep the building's heritage intact. At the same time, we had to guarantee the strength and safety of the building. This example demonstrates how failure to execute plans can lead to disaster, even when the plan itself is sound on paper.

But what I learned from this project wasn't the importance of careful execution, but also the role of raw action in fixing what's broken. When I took over the project, I didn't have the luxury of starting from scratch. We had to act quickly to stabilize the structure before it collapsed entirely. That required raw action–getting on-site immediately, assessing the damage firsthand, and making quick decisions about how to proceed, even before we had a fully revised plan. It was messy, it was stressful, but that raw action bought us the time we needed to execute the repairs properly. This combination of raw action and careful execution saved the project and preserved a piece of Sardinian history.

The Science of Action: Why Raw Action Works

Raw action might seem reckless, but it's backed by science. Psychologists have found that taking action, even imperfect action, can break the cycle of procrastination and doubt, a phenomenon known as the 'action bias'. When I jumped into that door-to-door outreach after losing a contract, I was acting on instinct, but I was also activating my brain's reward system. Studies show that taking action releases dopamine, a neurotransmitter that boosts motivation and makes us feel accomplished, even if the action is small. That initial burst of dopamine gave me the momentum I needed to keep going, eventually leading to a more refined execution.

Refined execution, on the other hand, engages the brain's prefrontal cortex, the part responsible for planning, decision-making, and attention to detail. When I revised the structural calculations for the Campidanese house, I was using my prefrontal cortex to ensure quality and safety. The combination of raw action and refined execution leverages both the emotional and rational parts of the brain, creating a powerful synergy that drives success.

The Raw-to-Refined Cycle: Combining Action and Execution

That Campidanese house project taught me that execution isn't a single step, it's a process that often starts with raw action and evolves into refined execution. I've combined these two forces into the 'raw-to-refined cycle'. This cycle uses the dynamic interplay between the raw energy to start and the careful execution to finish.

Raw Action – Start with Grit: Begin with raw, unpolished action–the kind of bold, gritty effort that gets you moving, even if it's imperfect. For me, this meant jumping into the Campidanese house project immediately, taking quick action to stabilize the structure before it was too late. In your life, it might mean making a cold call, starting a project with limited resources, or taking a risk without overthinking it. The goal is to break through inertia and create momentum.

Refined Execution – Build with Precision: Once you've gained momentum, shift to refined execution–careful, deliberate action that ensures quality and longevity. For me, this meant revising the structural calculations, replacing the beams, and using the right materials to complete the Campidanese house project. In your life, it might mean fine-tuning your project, seeking feedback, or perfecting your approach. The goal is to turn your initial spark into a lasting result.

Reflect and Iterate – Learn and Improve: After executing, take time to reflect on what worked and what didn't, then iterate to improve. For me, this meant learning from the mistakes of the previous company and ensuring I never repeated them in future projects. In your life, it might mean evaluating your results, adjusting your strategy, and applying those lessons to your next endeavor. The goal is to grow with every cycle, becoming a better builder with each project.

This cycle has guided me through countless projects, from small repairs to large commercial builds.

Applying the Raw-to-Refined Cycle: A Practical Exercise

To help you combine raw action and refined execution in your own life, here's a simple exercise I use whenever I need to turn an idea into reality: The Action-Execution Challenge. This exercise takes just a few minutes, but it can help you get started and follow through with precision.

Raw Action (2 minutes): Write down one idea or goal you've been hesitant to start. Then, identify one raw, unpolished action you can take right now to get moving–no overthinking. For example: "I want to start a new project–I'll email a potential collaborator today." Commit to doing it within the next 24 hours.

Refined Execution (2 minutes): After taking your raw action, write down one step you can take to refine your approach with care and precision. For example: "I'll research the collaborator's past projects and tailor my pitch to their needs." Schedule a time to complete this step within the next week.

Reflect and Iterate (1 minute): Once you've executed your refined step, reflect on what worked and what didn't. Write down one lesson you can apply to your next action. For example: "I learned that researching the collaborator made my pitch more effective—I'll do more research next time."

I used this exercise when I took on the Campidanese house project. My raw action was jumping in to stabilize the structure; my refined execution was revising the calculations and materials; and my reflection helped me improve my approach for future projects. Try it for yourself. It's a powerful way to turn your ideas into reality, one step at a time.

Conclusion: Execution is What Separates Success from Failure

Ultimately, the difference between those who realize their dreams and those who remain trapped in the desire to realize them lies in execution. The idea is fundamental, but it is the ability to act, starting with raw, gritty action and following through with refined execution, that will lead you to success. Do not let your projects, your vision, remain only on paper. Build them, step by step, with the right execution, and you will see how they transform into a solid and lasting reality.

19

The Inspection: Holding Yourself Accountable

"At the end of the day, we are accountable to ourselves—our success is a result of what we do." Catherine Pulsifer

In construction, a master builder never takes shortcuts or assumes that a structure will stand just because it looks solid on the surface. Every construction project undergoes a rigorous inspection process throughout the build to ensure that every element, from the foundation to the finishing touches, is built to last.

The same principle applies to success in life. If you do not regularly inspect your own actions, discipline, and progress, small flaws will quietly creep in, and before you know it, what you've built will begin to crumble. Accountability is often misunderstood as merely the process of reporting or answering to others for one's actions but holding *yourself* accountable is your personal inspection process and is what ensures your standards are maintained, your goals stay on track, and your results are as strong as the foundation you've laid. Accountability is a deeper, more transformative principle. It is the ability to own your actions–whether they lead to success or failure and the awareness that every decision you make has a direct impact on the outcome of your business or life.

Why Accountability Matters in Business

In business, accountability operates on multiple levels. At the most basic level, it ensures that targets are met, deadlines are respected, and resources are managed effectively. However, it goes far beyond this transactional level. Accountability is about creating a culture of performance and trust, both within yourself and your team. Without accountability, goals become mere aspirations, and plans are rendered useless.

Accountability serves as the glue that binds your business operations together. Without it, the components of your business, your team, your systems and your projects will fall apart. You cannot expect to build a thriving business without holding yourself and your team accountable for results.

As a business leader, if you consistently take accountability for your actions, you create an environment where others feel empowered to do the same. When everyone within an organization or team is accountable, the entire business operates at a higher level of integrity and productivity. Holding people accountable ensures that standards are met consistently. Effective leaders understand that accountability is not micromanaging or scrutinizing every decision made by their team. It's not being harsh but upholding a culture of excellence and responsibility.

The Daily Inspection – Checking Your Work

In construction, an inspector's job is to evaluate the work at every stage of the process, not just at the end. They ensure everything is aligned and properly constructed. The same goes for you. If you only assess your performance after a failure or setback, you're missing the point. The most successful builders and people inspect their work regularly, keeping track of their efforts, habits, and results.

Make self-inspection a daily practice. Ask yourself:

- Did I give my best effort today?

- Did I stay disciplined, or did I compromise?

- Did I honor my commitments to myself and others?

- Where did I lose focus or waste time?

By inspecting yourself daily, you prevent small cracks from developing into major problems. If there's an issue with your work, it's far easier to correct it early on than to wait for it to snowball into something far harder to fix.

Catch the Cracks Early – Fix Problems Before They Grow

In construction, a slight misalignment at the beginning of a project can lead to disastrous consequences if left uncorrected. The same holds true for your personal development. If you don't catch weaknesses and mistakes early, they'll grow into bigger, more challenging problems down the road.

The best way to prevent problems from getting out of hand is to recognize them before they escalate. Think about how you can address these weaknesses in real time, rather than letting them fester.

Small excuses, like skipping a workout or putting off a crucial task, can snowball into bad habits.

Minor lapses in integrity, such as justifying a small lie or taking a shortcut, can undermine your character.

Tolerating mediocrity by accepting "good enough" instead of pushing for excellence leads to a life of regret.

The sooner you spot these cracks, the easier it is to repair them. Commit to making improvements in real-time so you can ensure your foundation remains strong.

The Self-Auditor's Mindset – Be Brutally Honest

In construction, an inspector must be objective and unyielding. If a building is not up to code, it's not up to code, no matter how much the builder wants it to be. Likewise, if you're lying to yourself about your progress or effort, you're only sabotaging your future success.

A successful individual is their own toughest critic. Make a commitment to be brutally honest with yourself in every area of your life. Don't settle for comfort and don't make excuses.

Consider these questions:

- "I worked hard today." Did you really? Or did you take shortcuts?

- "I'm making progress." Or are you just treading water, avoiding the real challenges?

- "I deserve a break." Or are you procrastinating and avoiding the hard work that needs to be done?

A true inspector doesn't let emotion or desire for comfort influence their evaluation. Be ruthlessly honest with yourself, making sure you're building something that will stand the test of time and not just your pride.

Building Accountability into Your Business

In your business, accountability must be more than just a concept; it must be a practice that is incorporated into every decision-making process. Every meeting, every project plan, and every objective must be framed within the context of accountability. By doing so, you transform accountability from a buzzword into a powerful tool for operational excellence.

One of the most effective ways to build accountability is by setting clear, measurable goals. Whether you are managing a team or running a solo venture, goal setting provides the framework for evaluating progress. Without clear goals, it's impossible to measure success or failure. Without measurement, there is no need for accountability.

Another way to instill accountability in your business is through regular performance reviews and feedback mechanisms. These don't have to be formal or cumbersome, but they must be consistent. Honest, constructive feedback, both positive and negative–reinforces the importance of being accountable for your actions. In a high performing organization, these evaluations become a valuable tool for growth, not criticism.

Accountability Partners – External Inspectors for Your Life

Even the best builders don't inspect their own work alone. They bring in expert inspectors to double-check everything, ensuring that nothing is overlooked. In life, you need the same system: people who will hold you accountable and keep you to the highest standard.

The power of external accountability lies in the fact that it taps into your social nature. As humans, we are wired to seek connection, support, and approval from others. By setting up accountability with someone else, you tap into this natural tendency to meet the expectations of those around you. It creates a sense of urgency and a heightened awareness of your commitments. The simple act of telling someone about your goals can increase your commitment to those goals because you've made them real and shared them with another person. The fear of letting someone else down, or the desire to show progress, creates a strong internal drive to follow through.

Find accountability partners who won't let you settle for mediocrity or excuses. Surround yourself with individuals who challenge you, encourage you, and demand more from you.

Consider these types of accountability partners:

• A mentor who has already built what you want to build.

Mentorship is one of the most powerful ways to implement external accountability. A mentor is someone who has more experience and insight than you, and their role is not only to provide advice, but also to hold you accountable for the actions you take toward your goals. A mentor will ask the hard questions, challenge your assumptions, and provide the necessary feedback to keep you on track. Their perspective, based on experience, can also help you avoid mistakes and navigate obstacles more effectively.

• A peer or business partner who pushes you forward and holds you to your commitments.

• A coach who keeps you disciplined and ensures you're making progress.

- Your team or colleagues. In a business context, creating a culture of mutual accountability within your team can have a transformative effect. When each team member knows that they are accountable not just to their own performance but also to the success of the group, they are more likely to stay focused and motivated. This mutual commitment is what drives collective success. I have always believed in fostering an environment of shared accountability, where each person understands that their actions contribute to the broader goals of the team. In this setting, the success or failure of one person affects everyone, creating a unified, motivating force.

- Or even a community or team of like-minded individuals.

Choose people who won't just tell you what you want to hear. They should challenge you to level up. When others hold you accountable, it becomes much easier to stay on track and reach your highest potential.

The most significant benefit of leveraging external accountability is that it helps you stay committed. There will inevitably be times when motivation wanes or when you face challenges that make it tempting to quit. External accountability acts as a reminder of your commitments and helps you push through difficult moments. When you know someone is expecting progress from you, or when you have a standing appointment to report on your progress, it creates an inherent discipline that you might not otherwise have. This added layer of commitment not just to yourself but to others significantly reduces the chance of procrastination and helps you stay consistent in your efforts.

It's also important to note that accountability can work both ways. Mutual accountability fosters a deeper connection and trust among team members or between a mentor and mentee. When both parties are holding each other accountable, it creates a partnership based on respect and support. This doesn't mean you need someone to manage your every move, but simply having that understanding that someone else is invested in your success can provide the right nudge to keep you going, even when things get tough.

The Final Test – Can Your Life Withstand Pressure?

In construction, a building must pass a final, rigorous stress test before it's considered complete. It needs to endure extreme pressures, weight, wind, earthquakes, and more. In the same way, the true test of your growth and standards isn't how you perform when things are easy, but how you handle adversity and pressure.

- When life gets tough, will you fold, or will you stand firm?

- Do you stay disciplined when everything is falling apart?

- Do you push forward, or do you look for excuses to take it easy?

- Do you maintain your integrity, or do you make compromises when it's convenient?

Stress reveals whether the work you've done is solid or merely a facade. Many people crumble under pressure because they've never done the work to build a strong foundation. If you commit to holding yourself accountable every single day, however, you will be able to weather any storm that comes your way.

Conclusion: Live Like a Master Builder

A great constructor doesn't just hope the building will stand, they *know* it will. Why? Because they've meticulously inspected every detail, corrected every flaw, and ensured that every brick is laid with precision. They don't leave anything to chance. If you want to create success that lasts, you must adopt the same mindset. You must become the master builder of your own life.

This means inspecting your life with the same rigor and attention to detail that a builder uses to inspect a structure. It means identifying weaknesses, whether in your habits, your mindset, or your relationships, and addressing them immediately. Small cracks, if ignored, can turn into major structural failures. A single weak beam can compromise the integrity of an entire building. The same is true for your life.

To live like a master builder is to hold yourself to the highest standard. It's taking full accountability for every decision, every action, and every outcome.

PART FOUR

BUILDING RELATIONSHIPS AND LEADERSHIP

20

Mastering Communication

"The art of communication is the language of leadership." James Humes

In both construction and business, the ability to communicate effectively can make the difference between success and failure. Communication is more than conveying information; it's ensuring the message is understood and that it resonates with the audience. Over the years, I have learned that mastering communication is a vital skill that goes beyond speaking and listening. It encompasses clarity, emotional intelligence, and adaptability.

My communication style has refined through direct experience with thousands of clients, employees, and collaborators. In a field like construction and architecture, every person has different needs and expectations, requiring a significant degree of adaptability. As well as understanding practical needs, communication is also recognizing emotions, insecurities, and personal visions. When dealing with these situations daily, I learned to relate to a wide range of personalities, developing an empathetic, direct, and targeted communication style.

The most complex situations often occurred with couples. Internal dynamics could turn seemingly simple decisions, such as choosing the bathroom's color or the placement of an electrical outlet, into battlegrounds, often accompanied by heated and sometimes surreal arguments. I've witnessed major fights on site, where my role turned into that of a "builder psychologist" ready to mediate between the parties, calm tensions, and guide the conversation towards a shared solution. Often, what seemed like a technical disagreement was actually the desire of each party to see their own taste and vision represented in the project. The key was understanding these nuances and creating a space for dialogue where both parties felt heard.

In addition to clients, there were employees to manage—large teams working on multiple projects simultaneously. This required clear and motivating communication to maintain productivity and ensure every detail was meticulously attended to. Then, there were the relationships with banks, often complex and delicate, where it was essential to be clear and persuasive to obtain the best financing conditions. Suppliers, on the other hand, required ongoing negotiations to secure quality materials at the right price and on time, while other professionals–architects, engineers, interior designers–needed constant dialogue to maintain project coherence.

All these interactions taught me that effective communication isn't solely transmitting technical information, but listening, understanding, mediating, and inspiring trust. It was this combination of empathy, firmness, and relationship management that allowed me to build successful projects and establish solid, lasting relationships with everyone involved, even in the most delicate and complex situations.

The Role of Communication in Leadership

As a leader in construction and business, communication is at the core of building trust and influencing others. The way you communicate directly impacts your relationships with clients, employees, partners, and stakeholders. In my early years, I observed the influence that clear, concise communication had on getting things done efficiently, especially in high-pressure situations where deadlines and budgets were tight.

Leaders must articulate their vision, expectations, and goals in a way that inspires action. For example, when managing a large construction project, a miscommunication regarding a specific detail can result in costly delays or errors. Effective communication can prevent these pitfalls and keep everyone on the same page.

Building Trust through Clear Communication

One of the first lessons I learned in business was that communication builds trust. Trust is essential in any relationship, but it is particularly important in construction, where the stakes are high and the work is physically demanding. Clients need to trust that you will deliver on your promises, that your team will execute the project to the highest standards, and that issues will be resolved quickly and transparently.

Early in my career, I had to work hard to build this trust. For example, when dealing with a complicated client who had high expectations, I made sure to be transparent at every stage of the project. I explained any potential setbacks, provided updates on progress, and actively listened to their concerns. This open line of communication helped to establish credibility, and the client became a loyal supporter of our work.

Effective Listening: The Cornerstone of Communication

A common misconception is that effective communication is all about speaking well, but listening is just as important. To lead effectively, you must be an active listener.

Listening attentively to clients allows you to better understand their needs and concerns, which can then be addressed proactively. For example, when a client expressed concerns about the cost of a project, I didn't immediately dismiss their worries. Instead, I took the time to listen, ask questions, and offer solutions that would meet their budget without compromising quality. This approach not only resolved the issue, but also strengthened our working relationship.

Even when working with the team, listening is key. By welcoming their feedback, you can identify areas for improvement and make adjustments that lead to better performance. Showing the team that their opinions matter and that you value their contributions creates a motivating and collaborative environment.

Adapting Your Communication Style

Another essential aspect of communication is adaptability. People have different communication preferences and styles, and being able to adjust your approach accordingly can improve the outcome of interactions. In construction, for example, you might communicate with a highly technical architect, a hands-on project manager, or a client with little experience in construction. Each of these individuals will require a different communication approach.

In my experience, when talking to technical professionals, I focus on the details, being specific and precise with terminology. However, with clients, especially those not familiar with construction terms, I simplify my language and focus on the big picture, helping them understand the value they're getting without overwhelming them with jargon.

The ability to adapt your communication style is not just about changing how you speak; it's also about how you listen. Some people prefer direct, concise communication, while others may need more background information to feel comfortable with decisions. By recognizing these differences and adapting accordingly, you not only get the information across with clarity, but also demonstrate respect for others' preferences, fostering stronger relationships and more effective collaborations.

Non-Verbal Communication: The Unsung Hero

While verbal communication is often the focus, non-verbal communication plays an equally important role in conveying messages. Body language, facial expressions, posture, and tone of voice all provide valuable cues that either reinforce or contradict what is being said.

In construction, where face-to-face interactions are common, non-verbal communication is essential. If you are leading a meeting with a team of workers or discussing plans with a client, the tone of your voice and your body language can set the tone for the entire conversation. A confident posture and a calm tone can reassure your team during high-stress situations, while an open posture can encourage collaboration and engagement.

Throughout my career, I've realized that a great deal of communication happens without words. A firm handshake, maintaining eye contact, or simply nodding to acknowledge someone's input can go a long way in building rapport and fostering a positive working environment.

Conflict Resolution Through Communication

Business projects often come with their fair share of conflicts, like disagreements between workers, misunderstandings with clients, or even external factors. The ability to resolve these conflicts effectively requires strong communication skills. Often, conflicts arise due to poor communication or misinterpretation of information.

In these situations, I've learned the importance of remaining calm and approaching the issue with a problem-solving mindset. Rather than focusing on blame, I aim to address the root cause of the issue through open dialogue. For instance, when a scheduling conflict arose on a project, instead of getting frustrated, I sat down with the parties involved, listened to their concerns, and collaboratively worked towards a solution. This type of communication diffused tension and ensured the project stayed on track.

Communicating with Purpose and Intent

Ultimately, the most effective communication is intentional. Every conversation, whether with a client, a team member, or a business partner, should have a clear purpose. Without purpose, communication can become scattered, confusing, and ineffective.

Before entering a conversation, I take a moment to reflect on the outcome I want to achieve. Whether it's resolving a problem, making a decision, or simply clarifying expectations, having a clear purpose ensures that my message is directed and impactful. This focused approach helps prevent miscommunication and keeps conversations on track.

Conclusion

Mastering communication is an ongoing journey. It's a dynamic skill that requires practice, reflection, and a willingness to adapt. Over the years, I have learned that communication is not simply about exchanging words, but about fostering understanding, building relationships, and inspiring action. The ability to communicate effectively is what sets great leaders apart from the rest. As you continue to grow in your career and personal life, investing in mastering communication will pay dividends in every aspect of your journey.

21

Laying the Foundations for Relationships That Build Success

"Your success is not determined by what you know, but by who you connect with and how you collaborate. Build relationships that elevate, and the rest will follow." Mr. Ibba

Success isn't a solitary pursuit; it's a collective one. Behind every great achievement, there's often a network of people who have helped, supported, and collaborated with you along the way. The reality is that no matter how talented or knowledgeable you are, your success will always be heavily influenced by the people you choose to surround yourself with. If you want to reach the next level, the relationships you build with peers, clients, collaborators, or partners will make all the difference.

In this chapter, we explore the importance of relationships and how they are the cornerstone of personal and professional growth.

Building the right relationships is an ongoing journey, one that requires effort, strategy, and intentionality.

In 40 years of work, I have renovated homes for entire generations: first for the parents, then for the children, and finally for the grandchildren. This was possible because I established trusting relationships with my clients. A fundamental aspect is always being available. I remember an episode from my younger years: on a rainy night with thunderstorms and a blackout, a man called me in desperation because his wife was unwell and needed help with the electricity. His maintenance worker did not answer, so he turned to me. He was not yet my client, but I went immediately and fixed the problem. From that day on, we worked together for over 20 years. Trust is built through forging relationships, concrete actions and genuine availability, and that is what makes the difference in the long run.

The Power of Networking: More Than Just Connections

Networking often gets a bad reputation for being superficial, transactional, and based purely on the exchange of business cards or LinkedIn endorsements. But true networking is about much more than that. It's about building genuine relationships based on shared values, trust, and mutual respect.

Networking is an art form. It involves the ability to connect with others on a personal level while finding ways to provide value. It can encompass giving advice, sharing resources, or simply lending a hand when needed. Effective networking demonstrates not only your expertise but also your reliability and willingness to contribute. By giving as much as receiving, you create a positive reputation for yourself, one that signals that you are a person others want to do business with, collaborate with, and trust. Networking should feel like building a community of like-minded individuals who share a common goal and vision. This network will become your support system during difficult times and a source of opportunities as you grow and expand.

The people you network with today could become partners, collaborators, or even lifelong friends tomorrow.

The Role of Social Capital in Business Success

In addition to your tangible assets, like skills, knowledge, and expertise, the network of relationships you maintain plays an essential role in your long-term success. This is known as social capital and is the goodwill and trust you build within your community.

Just as financial capital can be used to invest in your business, social capital can be leveraged to open doors, gain support, and attract new opportunities. This might be through a recommendation from a trusted colleague or an introduction to a potential investor. The more you build and invest in relationships, the more social capital you accumulate. And just like any form of capital, it needs to be nurtured and maintained over time.

Your network is not just a collection of names on a list, but a dynamic system of relationships that requires ongoing investment. Whether it's checking in with an old business partner, offering support to a colleague, or simply taking the time to reach out to someone you haven't spoken to in a while, these seemingly small acts of connection are what build your social capital and create a foundation for future opportunities.

Building Strong Relationships in Your Industry: The Key to Long-Term Success

In any industry, the relationships you build with your peers, clients, and competitors can determine your success or failure. You are not working in a vacuum. Your business thrives on the collaboration, support, and trust of those around you. In every aspect of your work, you will find that relationships with those in your field open doors to new ideas, resources, and avenues for growth, creating a network of people who trust you, value your contributions, and want to see you succeed.

When you connect with people in your industry, you build a community of professionals who can provide you with insights, guidance, and opportunities. This network can offer different perspectives on challenges you may face, and their support can be instrumental in finding solutions.

In addition to networking within your industry, it is important to stay abreast of industry trends and developments. By attending conferences, workshops, and events, you can continue to build connections while staying informed about shifts in the market. This ongoing learning process will allow you to position yourself as a thought leader, someone others can turn to for advice and guidance.

Client Relationships: Building Trust and Loyalty

In business, particularly in industries like construction, design, and other service-based sectors, your relationship with clients is a direct reflection of the success of your business. Your clients are the lifeblood of your company. If they trust you and feel valued, they will not only become repeat clients, but will also refer you to others.

In a highly competitive market, it's the relationships you form with clients that often set you apart from your competitors. It's not just about the work you do, but the way you make your clients feel throughout the process. Consistent communication, regular check-ins, and a commitment to delivering on promises will ensure that your clients return to you time and time again.

Building strong relationships with clients requires you to listen to their needs, provide solutions that meet those needs, and communicate with transparency and respect. Clients want to feel heard, understood, and respected. By establishing trust, you lay the foundation for long-lasting partnerships that go beyond just a transactional exchange.

A key element in building client relationships is understanding the power of follow-up. Never underestimate the impact of a thank-you email, a check-in call, or a post-project review. These small gestures can go a long way in keeping the relationship alive and ensuring that the client feels valued beyond the completion of a job. Building trust with clients means being accessible, transparent, and reliable throughout the entire project, from start to finish.

Trust is the most valuable currency in life and business. It takes years to build, seconds to break, and a lifetime to repair. Whether dealing with clients, employees, business partners, or personal relationships, your reputation and the trust others place in you determine the opportunities that come your way. A solid reputation is not something you can buy, it is earned through consistent actions, integrity, and reliability. In a world where people are quick to judge and slow to forgive, protecting your credibility should be a top priority.

The Power of Trust in Business and Life

Trust is the foundation of every successful relationship. It creates loyalty, reduces friction in decision-making, and fosters long-term partnerships. When people trust you, they believe in your words, rely on your judgment, and feel secure working with you.

In life and business, nothing is more valuable than a solid reputation built on trust. It attracts opportunities, creates meaningful relationships, and opens doors that money cannot buy. Trust is not about what you say it is about what you do, consistently, over time. Defend it fiercely, protect it with integrity, and use it to build a legacy that lasts.

Why Trust Matters:

Generates Repeat Business – In any industry, a trustworthy reputation ensures that customers return and recommend you to others.

Builds Strong Teams – Employees thrive under the guidance of honest, fair, and reliable leaders.

Fosters Deeper Relationships – In personal life, trust is what makes bonds unbreakable.

Enhances Credibility – Whether you are selling a service or an idea, people listen when they trust the source. When trust is present, everything flows more smoothly. When it is absent, even the simplest interactions become difficult.

How to Build Trust and Protect Your Reputation

Trust is not given, it is earned through developing a relationship and actions, such as consistency and honesty.

Always Keep Your Word – Nothing destroys trust faster than broken promises. Whether it is a verbal agreement or a signed contract, your word must be as good as gold. If you commit to something, follow through, no excuses.

Be Transparent and Honest – People appreciate honesty, even when the truth is uncomfortable. Acknowledge your mistakes, admit when you do not have the answers, and communicate openly. Transparency prevents misunderstandings and strengthens credibility.

Consistency Is Key – Trust is built over time. You cannot be reliable one day and unpredictable the next. Remain consistent in your work ethic, decisions, and personal integrity, that's what makes people trust you.

Do the Right Thing, Even When No One Is Watching – How you treat people when there is nothing to gain speaks volumes about your values. Your reputation is what people say about you when you are not in the room. Make sure it is something positive.

Take Responsibility, Not Just Credit – When things go wrong, take ownership. People respect leaders who accept responsibility rather than shift blame. At the same time, share the credit when things go well. Trust grows when people feel valued and recognized.

Go Above and Beyond – One of the simplest ways to build a strong reputation is to exceed expectations. Take that extra step. People remember those who go the extra mile.

Be Mindful of Your Associations – Your reputation is also influenced by the company you keep. Surround yourself with reliable individuals and avoid those who act dishonestly or make last-minute decisions. If you associate with someone who has a bad reputation, it will reflect on you as well.

Rebuilding Trust After It Has Been Damaged

No one is perfect, and sometimes trust is broken. When that happens, how you handle the situation determines whether you will repair or destroy your reputation.

How to Restore Trust:

Acknowledge The Mistake – Denying or hiding a failure makes things worse.

Apologize Sincerely – A genuine apology includes taking responsibility and showing remorse.

Make Amends – Actions speak louder than words; demonstrate your commitment to fixing the issue.

Be Patient – Rebuilding trust takes time. Stay consistent in proving that you have changed.

Losing trust is easy, but regaining it requires humility, honesty, and continuous effort.

Building Resilience Through Relationships: Support System Equal Strength in Numbers

As you advance in your career or business, one thing becomes increasingly clear: you cannot do it all on your own. While the work may be yours to do, building a support system is key to long-term success. Surrounding yourself with a group of trusted individuals who can help you navigate challenges, provide feedback, and offer advice will provide the strength you need to keep pushing forward.

Support systems take many forms: close friends, trusted business partners, industry peers, or even family members who understand your goals and are there to lend a helping hand when things get tough. These are the people who lift you up when you're down, offer constructive criticism when needed, and celebrate your successes with you. Their support will not only help you stay focused on your goals, but will also allow you to recover quickly from setbacks.

Building a support system isn't relying on others to solve your problems, but creating a network of people who can offer perspectives, guidance, and encouragement when needed. It's knowing that you have people who believe in you and are willing to walk with you through the ups and downs of life and business. The resilience that comes from having a strong support system can help you stay grounded and maintain the confidence you need to tackle any challenge.

Reflection: Consider your current relationships, both personal and professional. Which ones are you nurturing, and which ones need more attention? What steps can you take today to start building deeper, more meaningful connections that will help propel you forward?

Sales and Marketing as Relationship Building

In order to sell your products or services, it's vital to know your audience. Understanding the needs, fears, and desires of your audience is crucial to creating a marketing message that resonates with them.

In a digital world, content is one of the most powerful tools for attracting and retaining customers. Creating relevant, valuable content is essential for building a relationship with the customer.

Sales should be seen as a way to build long-term relationships with customers. Using a consultative approach, listening to customer needs, and offering tailored solutions leads to more satisfied and loyal customers.

Conclusion: Building Bridges to Success

Success is never a solo journey; it's a journey made possible by the people you connect with along the way.Building the right relationships is one of the most valuable investments you can make in your personal and professional journey. By focusing on networking, collaborating with peers, fostering strong client relationships, and creating a solid support system, you create a network of support that will help you scale your business, achieve your goals, and ultimately, build the life and legacy you desire.

22

The Art of Negotiation

"You must never try to make all the money that is in a deal. Let the other fellow make some money too, because if you have a reputation for always making all the money, you won't have many deals." J. Paul Getty

Negotiation is not just a skill; it's an art. It's about understanding people, managing conflict, and navigating conversations toward mutually beneficial outcomes. Whether you're securing contracts, forging partnerships, resolving disputes, or working on personal agreements, the principles of negotiation apply to every area of life and business. In construction, effective negotiation can make the difference between a successful project and a failed one. But beyond the job site, negotiation is the cornerstone of every relationship, whether in business, family, or friendships. Mastering the art of negotiation requires not only the ability to advocate for your own interests but also the capacity to understand the needs and desires of others.

A Personal Story: Negotiating Through a Crisis

One of the most challenging and pivotal negotiations I've ever faced happened while I was building a hotel. The project was a large-scale development, one that had great potential, and I had invested a lot of my resources and time into making it a reality. But halfway through the build, things took an unexpected turn that tested my skills, patience, and resolve.

The hotel was well underway, and we had a strong crew in place, but then I learned that the owner was running into serious financial trouble. The funds that were supposed to keep the project moving had run dry. As it turned out, the owner had trusted the engineer overseeing the project, but unfortunately, the engineer had seriously underestimated the costs involved in construction. There had been a lot of miscalculations, and it had left the owner in a position where he couldn't meet his financial commitments.

At the time, I had a choice to make. I could walk away, but that would have meant the collapse of the entire project and potentially a significant loss for all involved. Or, I could negotiate, not just with the owner but with the banks as well. It was a difficult decision because I knew I would need to maintain a delicate balance between securing funds, keeping the owner's trust, and ensuring the integrity of the entire project.

I remember sitting down with the owner in his office, which had become a tense space filled with worry and frustration. He was visibly upset, and I could tell this situation wasn't his fault.

He had put his trust in the engineer, and it had backfired. He wasn't looking to avoid his responsibilities, but the pressure of the situation was weighing heavily on him.

Negotiating with him wasn't about pushing for what I wanted; it was about finding a solution that could allow the project to continue and give him the breathing room he needed to get back on track. I understood that the owner was in a vulnerable position, and I didn't want to take advantage of that. So, we started by having an honest conversation. I laid out the reality of the costs, explained the mistakes made, and suggested a phased payment plan that could help him manage his finances more effectively.

The negotiation was tough, but it was built on mutual respect and understanding. After hours of back-and-forth, we found a middle ground. He would secure additional funding, but we needed to extend the deadlines and revise some of the payment terms.

But the negotiations didn't end there. I also had to negotiate with the banks to secure additional loans. The banks were naturally hesitant to release more funds, considering the situation at hand, but I knew that without their support, the project would grind to a halt. I gathered all the financial data, presented a revised cost breakdown, and made a strong case for why the hotel was still a viable investment. It wasn't easy, but after several rounds of discussions, we were able to secure the funding we needed.

Looking back, this negotiation was a defining moment in my career. It wasn't about just getting the best deal it was about making sure everyone involved could walk away with something positive. The owner trusted me to help him navigate the financial crisis, and in turn, I had to negotiate for the future of the project. I'm proud to say the hotel was completed successfully, and it turned out to be one of the best investments in my portfolio.

This experience taught me that negotiation is rarely about winning or losing. It's about finding solutions that work for everyone involved, even when the stakes are high. It's about listening, understanding the needs of others, and finding a way to collaborate through difficult circumstances. It was a reminder that the art of negotiation is about building long-term relationships, not just securing immediate wins.

Understanding the Fundamentals of Negotiation

At its core, negotiation is about reaching an agreement that satisfies all parties involved. It's a dynamic process, requiring a clear understanding of your goals, the other party's objectives, and the variables at play. To be effective, you must approach negotiation with an open mind and the flexibility to adapt as circumstances change.

One key principle of successful negotiation is knowing that it's not about getting everything you want, it's about finding a balance that allows both sides to feel they've achieved something of value. This principle applies whether you're securing a contract with a client, managing a dispute with a partner, or even navigating family decisions. In the construction industry, for example, the negotiation process is rarely one-sided. Clients may ask for budget cuts, but as a contractor, you need to balance their demands with the quality standards you uphold. The same happens in personal life whether it's a financial decision with a partner or a discussion with a friend, compromise and understanding are key to mutual satisfaction.

Real-World Examples of Successful Negotiations in Construction

In my years of experience in construction, I've been involved in numerous high-stakes negotiations that required both patience and strategy. One instance that stands out is when I was negotiating a large-scale residential project with a client who had a fixed budget. The scope of work was extensive, and we both knew that cutting costs could impact the quality of the final product.

I approached the negotiation with an understanding that the client's priorities were value for money and timely completion. My goal was to maintain the project's quality without exceeding the budget. Instead of viewing the negotiation as a battle, I positioned it as a collaborative discussion. We explored alternative materials that would achieve the same aesthetic but at a lower cost, and I offered flexible payment terms that allowed the client to manage their cash flow better.

In the end, both parties walked away feeling satisfied: the client received the quality they expected, and we secured the contract. This negotiation taught me the importance of building a relationship based on trust and mutual benefit. It wasn't just about the deal, it was about understanding the underlying needs of both parties and finding common ground.

This same principle holds true in business and life. Negotiating for a raise, securing a partnership, or even making a decision about a family vacation involves not just a desire to get your way, but a willingness to understand the other person's position. When you approach negotiations with empathy and flexibility, the outcome is more likely to benefit everyone involved.

Key Negotiation Techniques and Strategies

Mastering negotiation requires a combination of preparation, strategy, and adaptability. There are several techniques that can sharpen your negotiation abilities, whether in business or life.

Preparation is Everything

Before entering any negotiation, take the time to prepare thoroughly. In business, this means understanding the market, your value proposition, and the specifics of the deal at hand. For example, when negotiating with contractors, it's essential to have a clear understanding of labor costs, material prices, and the scope of work. In personal life, preparation might involve understanding your goals and boundaries, whether it's negotiating a budget with a spouse or discussing responsibilities with a family member. In both cases, being prepared shows that you value the process and the relationship. It also builds confidence. The more information you gather, the more leverage you have during the negotiation.

Active Listening

One of the most powerful tools in negotiation is the ability to listen. Often, people enter negotiations thinking only about what they want to say next. Instead, successful negotiators focus on understanding the other party's needs, desires, and potential concerns. In construction, this might involve listening carefully to a client's specifications and concerns, which could reveal potential cost-saving opportunities or areas where they're willing to compromise. Active listening in life is just as crucial. Whether it's a business partner or a family member, when you truly listen, you create an atmosphere of trust and respect, which makes it easier to reach an agreement.

Finding Common Ground

A successful negotiation always includes finding common ground. While you may not get everything you want, there's often a solution that satisfies both parties. For instance, in a construction project, you might agree to a smaller scope of work or a slightly higher price in exchange for a longer payment period. This concept of mutual benefit applies across all aspects of life. Whether you're negotiating with colleagues or loved ones, the key is finding a solution that everyone feels comfortable with.

Concession Strategy

Negotiation isn't about winning at all costs, it's about finding a fair compromise. Concessions are a natural part of the process. However, they should be strategic. When making concessions, make sure they align with your overall goals. For example, in business negotiations, you may offer a discount in exchange for a larger project or a longer-term contract. In personal negotiations, such as family decisions, you may agree to one person's preference in exchange for a future compromise on your own terms. The important point is that each concession should be reciprocated. This way, both parties feel as though they've gained something from the negotiation.

Know When to Walk Away

Not every negotiation will be successful, and it's essential to know when to walk away. In business, this means knowing your limits and not being afraid to walk away from a deal if it no longer serves your best interests. In life, it might mean knowing when a relationship or arrangement is no longer working, and it's time to seek a better path forward. Walking away is not a failure, it's a sign of strength and wisdom. It shows that you have clear boundaries and are willing to prioritize your values and goals.

Patience and Timing

Timing can make or break a negotiation. Whether you're in a construction contract negotiation or trying to reach an agreement on a family matter, patience is key. Rushing into decisions or making hasty concessions can lead to poor outcomes. Sometimes, stepping back and giving the other party space to reflect can lead to a better deal. In life, patience is just as crucial. Waiting for the right moment to propose a solution or make a request increases the likelihood of success. It's about knowing that not everything has to happen immediately–good things take time.

Sharpening Your Negotiation Skills: Practice and Reflection

Negotiation is a skill that improves with practice. The more you engage in negotiations, the better you'll become. Each negotiation provides an opportunity to learn, adapt, and refine your approach.

To sharpen your negotiation skills, regularly reflect on past negotiations. What worked? What didn't? What could you have done differently? This ongoing process of self-assessment will allow you to grow into a more skilled, effective negotiator. Furthermore, reading books, attending seminars, or participating in workshops on negotiation will expand your toolkit and give you new strategies to apply.

Conclusion: The Art of Negotiation in Business and Life

Mastering the art of negotiation isn't being manipulative, it's having mutual respect and finding solutions that benefit everyone involved. The principles of negotiation are preparation, active listening, flexibility, and a willingness to seek common ground. Successful negotiators understand that every conversation is an opportunity to build a relationship and create lasting value.

As you develop your negotiation skills, remember that each negotiation is not just an exchange of terms, but an exchange of trust, values, and long-term partnerships. By applying the techniques of negotiation with integrity and empathy, you'll build stronger relationships, close more successful deals, and create opportunities for growth both in business and in your personal life.

23

Leadership Built to Last

"Example is not the main thing in influencing others. It is the only thing." Albert Schweitzer

Leading by Example

Leadership goes far beyond directing others in the workplace. It is embodying the values, principles, and behaviors you wish to see in others. True leaders don't just tell people how things should be done; they show it through their actions, every day. Leading by example is not just a strategy for business success, but a principle that impacts every aspect of life. In both personal and professional spheres, it's the leader's actions that define their influence. Over the years, I've learned that the strongest, most enduring leadership comes not from a position of authority but from the ability to lead through integrity, empathy, and commitment.

The Power of Actions Over Words

I grew up in a family where there was little talking, and when we did speak, the main topic was work. There were no grand speeches. The only conversation topics were what to do next and how to do it. When there was a project to be completed, we did it, plain and simple. Once the goal was clarified, there was no need for further words: we moved to action. It was an attitude that was probably passed down through generations in my family: few questions, no unnecessary chatter.

As a child, I remember often observing my grandfather at work. I was curious and would ask questions, but his answer was always the same, in Sardinian: "*Castia e impara*" which means "Watch and learn." According to him, the best way to learn was to observe. Words were superfluous: action was what mattered.

This approach deeply shaped my way of being, both in life and at work. On the construction site or during a complex project, promises or explanations are not enough. A project can't be built by simply talking about it but requires hands-on effort, collaboration, and constant attention. Trust is built with actions, with the quality of the work, and with attention to detail. People are always watching: clients, employees, suppliers, and collaborators evaluate every move, every choice, and every result.

Over the years, I have applied this philosophy in managing interpersonal relationships and professional connections. I have learned that leadership is manifested through concrete actions:

solving problems, keeping promises, and acting decisively are the key elements to gaining respect and credibility. Even in moments of tension or conflict, remaining calm and demonstrating with actions the intention to find a solution has been my strength. What you do, how you handle adversity, and the values you live by resonate far more than any motivational speech.

When I first started my business, I noticed that the most respected leaders weren't the ones who gave orders from a distance. They were the ones who were there with their teams, leading from the front, sharing in both the successes and struggles. I made it a point to work alongside my team, showing them that no task was too small, no challenge too great. This became the foundation of a culture where respect wasn't just given, it was earned through consistent actions.

This attitude has also been useful in relationships with banks, suppliers, and other professionals. In our personal lives, leading by example applies to how we show up for our families, friends, and communities. If we expect our children to be respectful, compassionate, and diligent, we must first model those behaviors in our interactions with them and others. Leadership begins at home, in the way we treat the people closest to us. Our children, like our team members, are always watching, learning from the way we live our lives.

In all these situations, words can reassure, but only decisive and consistent action builds trust. The power of actions, deeply rooted in my upbringing, became the foundation of my work and life:

doing what you say and proving it with deeds has always been the best business card.

Leading with Vision and Purpose

Good leadership translates vision into reality. A leader holds a clear sense of purpose and helps others see that vision through their actions. When you lead by example, you aren't just going through the motions. You're actively pursuing a goal, a mission that inspires others to follow suit. A leader with a compelling vision doesn't just ask people to follow, they show them what's possible by making every decision in alignment with that vision.

Setting the Standard for Work Ethic and Values

Leadership starts with setting a standard not just for performance, but for values. The way we approach work, personal goals, and even our most routine tasks sets the tone for everyone around us. In construction, where I came to realize that every detail matters, this principle became invaluable. My team knew that when I asked for a standard of excellence, I wasn't just talking about results. I was asking for the effort and dedication required to get there. Excellence doesn't happen by accident, it's a mindset, a culture, and a relentless pursuit of the highest standards. This is something I've strived to instill in every project I've overseen. In construction, quality is everything; it's what sets you apart in a competitive industry.

By striving to be the best version of yourself–physically, emotionally, and intellectually, you show up as a role model, when interacting with both colleagues, friends, or family. Leading by example means having the right attitude, staying committed to personal growth, and demonstrating that success is a byproduct of consistent effort. When people see you dedicate yourself to your goals, they will be inspired to do the same.

Demonstrating Integrity

One of the most powerful aspects of leadership is integrity. In business, integrity is about delivering on promises, being transparent, and taking responsibility for mistakes. In life, integrity means staying true to your values, being honest in your relationships, and holding yourself accountable for your actions.

During a particularly challenging project, I faced a problem that could have jeopardized our deadline and client satisfaction. Instead of sweeping the issue under the rug or blaming others, I took full responsibility. I communicated openly with the client, explained the issue, and assured them of our commitment to resolve it. In return, we not only salvaged the project, but also built a stronger relationship based on trust and transparency.

This principle extends into every aspect of life. If you make a mistake in a personal relationship, the same integrity applies. Owning up to your mistakes, apologizing when necessary, and taking the right steps to make amends are key components of leadership in both business and life. Integrity is the foundation of long-term trust with all the people in your world.

Empathy in Leadership

Emotional intelligence is a trait that is useful in all relationships. True leadership not only encourages people to reach their potential; it also lifts them up, understanding their needs and supporting them when life gets tough. In construction, there have been times when my workers faced personal challenges that impacted their performance. As a leader, I knew that part of my role was to be there for them, not just in the professional capacity, but as a mentor and friend.

I've learned that empathy is a vital trait in leadership—to show up with a listening ear, offer support during difficult times, and be patient. It's about recognizing that everyone has their own story, and that success is built not only on skill and effort but on the ability to connect with people.

In life, empathy creates deeper, more meaningful relationships. It's the foundation for trust, understanding, and mutual respect.

Improving Emotional Intelligence

Emotional intelligence is a skill that develops over time and requires consistent effort and practice. One of its key pillars is self-awareness, which allows us to monitor our emotions and understand how they influence our behavior. When we are aware of our emotions, we can respond more thoughtfully and less impulsively. This is the first step toward improving our relationships, both personal and professional.

Emotional regulation is equally crucial. Learning to manage our instinctive reactions and avoid them in stressful situations is essential for preventing conflicts and misunderstandings. The ability to stay calm, even in tense moments, allows us to approach problems rationally and build stronger connections. When we are not overwhelmed by our emotions, we can respond with empathy and understanding rather than reacting defensively or aggressively.

Another vital aspect of emotional intelligence is active listening. To communicate effectively, it's important to truly listen to what the other person is saying, not only at a verbal level but also non-verbally. Facial expressions, body language, and tone of voice are all clues that can help us better understand others' emotions. Being able to recognize these signals and respond appropriately strengthens the bond and promotes more open and sincere communication.

Social skills are the bridge that connects us to others. Being able to interpret social dynamics, understand others' emotions, and adapt to different social situations are all competencies that are part of emotional intelligence. A person with high emotional intelligence knows how to create a positive atmosphere, motivate others, and resolve conflicts constructively. Effective communication is not only about what we say, but also how we say it and how we respond to what others communicate.

In summary, improving emotional intelligence means being more self-aware, learning to regulate our emotions, listening actively, and developing social skills to interact harmoniously with others. This personal growth not only enhances our relationships but also makes us more resilient in the face of life's challenges.

Delegation and Trusting Your Team

Delegation is one of the most powerful tools you have as a leader. Don't see it as relinquishing control but instead view it as empowering your team and creating a structure where everyone can contribute to the success of the business. By trusting your team, giving them the autonomy to make decisions, and providing the support they need, you create an environment where everyone thrives. When done right, delegation becomes the cornerstone of effective leadership and sustainable business growth.

The Transition from Doing Everything Yourself to Delegating Effectively

As an entrepreneur and business owner, one of the most significant transitions you'll face is the shift from doing everything yourself to building a team and delegating responsibilities. Early on, it's easy to fall into the trap of trying to handle every task, believing that no one else can do it as well as you. But as your business grows, you'll quickly realize that you cannot do it all. Effective delegation is the key to scaling your business, empowering your team, and ultimately achieving greater success.

At one time, I was juggling ten construction sites, managing family matters, and trying to handle everything on my own from client meetings to project management, from accounting to marketing. I felt like I was being pulled in every direction, and the constant pressure was overwhelming, thinking only I could do everything to the highest standard. I believed it was faster, easier, and more reliable to rely on myself. However, this mindset became unsustainable. As my business grew, I realized that if I wanted to scale and continue to deliver at a high level, I had to shift my approach.

Making the decision to delegate led to radical changes in both my life and business. I didn't just lighten my workload but put the right people in place to do the work that truly mattered. This shift in mindset and strategy led to the creation of SuperLuce, a business born from a team capable of managing tasks independently, with my support. Delegation allowed me to scale my business, and it was through this process that I saw not only my workload diminish but also the growth of a loyal, empowered team.

How Trust in Your Team is Essential for Scaling and Growth

The first step in effective delegation is recognizing the value that other team members can bring. Without trust, delegation becomes meaningless. You cannot expect your team to take ownership of their work and make decisions independently if you micromanage every step. My turning point came when I realized that no matter how skilled I was, there were others who were just as capable at handling specific tasks. Trust is the foundation for growth. By putting faith in your team, you allow them to shine and contribute to the success of the business. I had to learn to let go of my perfectionist tendencies and trust that others could handle specific responsibilities, sometimes better than I could. This was a difficult adjustment for me, as I had spent years being hands-on in every aspect of my business. But once I made the shift, the benefits became clear. This trust empowered my team and motivated them to take ownership of their roles, creating a more dynamic and collaborative work environment.

Trusting your team also builds loyalty. When your team members feel that you believe in their abilities, they are more likely to invest their time and energy into the business. This sense of ownership creates a motivated workforce, one that is aligned with your vision and dedicated to your company's success.

Practical Advice on How to Delegate Tasks, Trust Your People, and Avoid Micromanaging

While delegating is essential for growth, it's not always easy to get it right. Here's some practical advice based on my experiences to help you delegate effectively and avoid falling into the trap of micromanaging.

1. Start by Identifying What Only You Can Do

When you're overwhelmed with tasks, it's easy to want to delegate everything at once. However, not all tasks are created equal. Start by identifying which tasks only you can do–things that require your specific skills, vision, or decision-making. For everything else, consider who on your team is best equipped to handle it.

In my case, I realized that I needed to focus on strategic direction, business development, and building relationships. I delegated tasks such as project management, client communication, and administrative duties to trusted team members who had the expertise and passion for these areas.

2. Match the Right Person to the Right Task

Delegation is most effective when you match the right person to the right task. It's essential to understand your team members' strengths, weaknesses, and areas of expertise. Delegate based on their skills and interests and provide the resources they need to succeed.

For instance, I have team members who excel at design, others who are experts in project management, and some who thrive in client relations. When delegating, I always make sure to align the tasks with their individual strengths, ensuring the best results.

3. Set Clear Expectations and Provide the Right Tools

When delegating, be sure to set clear expectations. Ensure your team understands the desired outcome, timeline, and any specific requirements. This clarity will help prevent misunderstandings and miscommunications. Additionally, provide them with the right tools, resources, and support to do the job effectively.

For example, when delegating a project, I ensure that my team has access to the latest software and tools, and that they are well-versed in the company's processes and standards. This allows them to perform with confidence and competence.

4. Trust, But Check-In Regularly

Once you've delegated tasks, trust your team to get the job done. However, that doesn't mean you should leave them to their own devices entirely. Regular check-ins, whether through meetings, progress reports, or status updates–ensure that everything is on track without micromanaging. These check-ins provide an opportunity for feedback, problem-solving, and further support.

I found that weekly meetings, where we reviewed key tasks and upcoming projects, helped everyone stay aligned without creating a micromanaging atmosphere. It was a balanced approach that kept the team motivated and accountable.

5. Give Feedback and Recognize Effort

Delegation also involves providing constructive feedback. Celebrate achievements and recognize when things go well but also offer guidance when something goes wrong. Feedback should be supportive, not punitive. It should encourage growth and improvement.

I always make a point of recognizing my team's successes, whether it's completing a challenging project or exceeding expectations. Acknowledging their efforts boosts morale and reinforces their trust in you as a leader. This approach fosters a positive work environment where people feel valued and motivated to perform at their best.

6. Let Go of Perfectionism

One of the biggest hurdles in delegation is the fear that the work won't be done to your exact standards. Perfectionism can be a barrier to delegating effectively. It's essential to accept that things may not always be done exactly the way you would do them, but that doesn't mean the work is of a lower quality.

I learned to let go of my perfectionist tendencies and embrace the diverse approaches of my team. This allowed me to focus on higher-level tasks and also gave my team the space to innovate and find their own solutions. By trusting them, I often found that their results exceeded my expectations.

Conclusion

Leadership is not just giving out orders or instructions, it's being the embodiment of the values, actions, and behaviors that drive success. Whether in construction or any other walk of life, leading by example is the most powerful way to influence others. By setting the standard, demonstrating integrity, fostering excellence, and showing empathy, you inspire those around you to rise to the occasion.

As your business grows, delegation becomes a necessity for scaling effectively. This doesn't mean doing less work but doing the right work and ensuring that the right people are in place to take on the tasks that will drive your success. By mastering the art of delegation, you not only free up your time to focus on strategic growth, but also build a team that is motivated, empowered, and loyal to your vision.

As you continue to lead, remember that every action you take, every decision you make, and every way you show up in the world, is an opportunity to teach, guide, and inspire. In both business and life, the most powerful way to lead is not through words alone, but through actions that reflect the highest standard of who you are and who you want others to become.

24

Mentorship and Coaching: The Power of Guidance

"Nemo tam doctus est ut omnia scire possit, nemo tam indoctus ut nihil discere non possit."

"No one is so learned that he can know everything, nor so unlearned that he cannot learn something." Cicero's *De Officiis*

Success is never a solitary journey. Behind every successful person, there is guidance, support, and wisdom passed down by others. Whether in business, personal development, or life itself, having the right mentors can accelerate growth, prevent costly mistakes, and open doors to new opportunities.

Mentorship is not just about receiving guidance; it is also about giving back. The best leaders learn from those ahead of them and teach those who follow. The cycle of mentorship and coaching creates stronger businesses, communities, and personal relationships.

The Impact of Having Mentors

A good mentor saves you years of trial and error. They have already faced challenges, made mistakes, and discovered what works. Their knowledge is a shortcut to smarter and faster growth.

My First Mentor

I still remember how I met my first mentor by chance. Initially, I reached out to him as a potential client, never imagining that he would become a key figure in my life. Over time, our relationship transformed into something much deeper, a friendship and a guiding force that completely changed my way of seeing things. His impact was decisive, and without him, it would have taken me years to understand many fundamental lessons. His experience and vision opened my eyes to possibilities I had never seen before, proving just how powerful the guidance of a true mentor can be.

How Mentors Shape Your Success:

• They provide clarity – A mentor helps you see the bigger picture and focus on what truly matters.

• They challenge your thinking – Growth when someone pushes you beyond your comfort zone.

• They offer practical wisdom – Unlike theory, a mentor's advice comes from real-life experience.

• They hold you accountable – When someone believes in you, you work harder to meet their expectations.

• They expand your network – Many opportunities come not just from skills, but from connections.

In life, as in business, the right mentor can help you make better decisions, avoid common pitfalls, and unlock your full potential.

Finding the Right Mentor

The best mentors are not always who you expect. Sometimes they are bosses, colleagues, family members, or even people outside your industry. The key is to find someone whose values, experiences, and mindset align with your goals.

How to Find the Right Mentor:

Identify where you need guidance – Business? Leadership? Personal growth?

Look for someone who has already succeeded in that area – Learn from those who have walked the path.

Observe their actions, not just their words – The best mentors lead by example.

Build relationships naturally – Instead of asking, "Will you be my mentor?", focus on learning from them first.

Be a great mentee – Show initiative, respect their time, and act on their advice.

In business and life, learning from the right people can make the difference between struggling for years or achieving success faster.

Becoming a Mentor – The Power of Giving Back

True leadership is not just about personal success; it is about helping others succeed. Just as you have benefited from guidance, you have a responsibility to share your knowledge and experiences.

Why You Should Mentor Others:

- It solidifies your knowledge – Teaching others forces you to master what you know.

- It creates a legacy – True success is measured by the people you help along the way.

- It strengthens your leadership – A great mentor becomes a respected authority.

- It keeps you connected – Teaching others introduces you to new perspectives and insights.

- It builds a strong network – The people you mentor today may become your greatest allies tomorrow.

Truly successful people feel a natural drive to give back what they have learned. Sharing their story, experiences, and guidance is not just an act of generosity but a deep need to create a lasting impact.

The satisfaction that comes from helping another person grow and achieve their goals far surpasses any material reward. Money can provide comfort, but nothing compares to the transformation you can create in someone else's life.

Conclusion: The Power of Guidance – From my Grandfather's Wisdom to the Strength of Mentorship

It's true, I've always thought that my first mentor was that person I met almost by chance, a potential client who later became a friend and a key guide in my life. But if I think about it carefully, my first mentor, my true inspiration, was my grandfather.

My grandfather, with his quiet words and strong actions, taught me lessons I still carry with me today. He didn't need grand speeches: his actions spoke for him. He showed me the value of hard work, honesty, and dedication. He taught me that words only carry weight if they are backed by deeds. And above all, he instilled in me the importance of building something that lasts, not just for oneself, but for those who will come after.

This is the essence of mentorship: learning from those who came before us and, in turn, becoming a guide for those who will follow. It's not just about receiving advice or avoiding mistakes; it's about creating a cycle of growth that enriches everyone, mentors and mentees alike.

Mentorship is a gift that is both given and received. It's an opportunity to accelerate our journey, but also to leave a mark on the world. Whoever you are, whatever your goal, remember that you don't have to do it all alone. Find someone who inspires you, challenges you, and shows you paths you never imagined. And when you're ready, become a mentor yourself. Because true success isn't measured solely by what you achieve, but by the lives you touch and the people you help grow.

My grandfather didn't know what a "mentor" was in the modern sense of the word, but he was one to me in every way. And today, as I share what I've learned with others, I feel I'm honoring his legacy. Because mentorship isn't just about business or career: it's about humanity, connection, and shared growth.

So, if you want to grow, find a mentor. If you want to leave a mark on the world, become one. And remember: the most powerful lessons don't always come from books or speeches, but from actions, examples, and the quiet wisdom of those who, like my grandfather, knew that true teaching is living with integrity and passion.

25

Strategic Partnerships

"If you want to go fast, go alone. If you want to go far, go together."
African Proverb

Strategic partnerships are not mere contractual collaborations. They are structural pillars that allow a business to withstand market shocks, enhance operational capabilities, and access new opportunities more efficiently. The ancient African proverb encapsulates a concrete truth: no entrepreneur can achieve sustainable and scalable growth without a solid ecosystem of strategic alliances. In a competitive and constantly evolving landscape, building strong partnerships is not optional it is an operational necessity.

Strategic partnerships represent a competitive advantage by combining resources, know-how, networks, and execution capabilities. This is not about seeking help in times of need, but about creating synergies that allow for faster, more precise, and more adaptable market responses. When critical resources such as skills, distribution channels, technologies, or production assets are shared, costs are reduced, lead times are shortened, and the value perceived by the end customer increases.

Trust and Alignment: The Foundations of Partnership

At the core of every effective alliance lie two non-negotiable elements: trust and alignment. Trust ensures operational continuity, even during uncertainty, while strategic alignment guarantees that actions remain coherent with shared objectives. Without these two components, any collaboration is destined to generate conflict, inefficiency, and wasted resources.

In the construction industry, where every mistake translates into delays, cost overruns, and disputes, selecting partners cannot be a random decision. A rigorous filter is required based on proven reliability, material quality, and alignment with company values. An effective partnership is not limited to meeting technical specifications; it is built upon a shared vision of quality, timing, and final outcomes.

Partnerships as Innovation Accelerators

Innovation does not emerge in a vacuum. It is the result of systemic interaction between diverse minds and competencies. Strategic partnerships provide the ideal environment for developing new, scalable, and market-responsive solutions. When companies with different specializations combine forces, they create favorable

Expanding the Network: A Strategic Approach

Building a network of partnerships doesn't happen by chance. It requires method, vision, and a clear plan for selecting, developing, and retaining key partners. A well-structured network enables rapid scaling, access to new markets, management of multidisciplinary projects, and diversification of both supply sources and demand channels.

These contacts can be nurtured into high-performance professional relationships. Every partner must be a strategic asset, selected based on measurable performance, proven reliability, and cultural compatibility. The goal is not to fill a list, but to create a value chain that enhances the overall competitiveness of the organization.

The Economic Impact of Strategic Partnerships

From a financial perspective, a well-structured partnership improves margins, reduces fixed costs, and increases speed to market. The integration of production, logistics, or design processes allows for both scale and scope economies, which directly impact the bottom line.

In construction, for example, working with reliable suppliers ensures continuity in deliveries, reduces waste, and enables smoother site management. Partnerships with strategic clients or agents can also open new business opportunities, promote

As a business grows, its needs evolve. Having long-term partners who can adapt, grow alongside the organization, and contribute to its transformation is a powerful competitive advantage. A well-maintained strategic alliance becomes an integral part of the business model, enhancing scalability, resilience, and innovation over time.

Conclusion: The Power of Strategic Partnerships

Strategic partnerships are structural pillars, not tactical tools but permanent components of the entrepreneurial project. Every solid alliance is a strategic choice that defines execution quality, innovation capacity, and the strength of future expansion.

Building partnerships means equipping oneself with the tools to manage market complexity, optimize internal resources, gain access to external expertise, and establish a presence in new segments. It's a process of selection, negotiation, verification, and continuous maintenance. When managed correctly, these alliances become part of a company's competitive advantage, contributing to the construction of a robust, responsive, and future-oriented enterprise.

PART FIVE

FACING CHALLENGES: BUILDING RESILIENCE AND INNOVATION

26

Resilience in Crisis: Building Through Adversity

"It is not the strongest of the species that survive, nor the most intelligent, but the one most responsive to change." Charles Darwin

In the world of construction and life, resilience and adaptability are essential. Building a business, a career, or a life from scratch means encountering setbacks, failures, and challenges along the way. The key to survival isn't about avoiding obstacles; it's about learning how to bounce back from them, stay flexible, and keep moving forward. My journey has been one of constant evolution, learning, and adapting, and it's these qualities, resilience and adaptability that have allowed me to overcome the toughest moments.

Personal Story

Looking back at my journey, resilience has been the thread that ties everything together. One of the earliest lessons in resilience came from my days as a young builder. On a project I was managing, a massive storm rolled in, causing delays and damage to the site. The pressure to meet deadlines was enormous, and at that moment, it felt like everything was falling apart. But instead of panicking, I took a step back and adapted. I reorganized the schedule, found solutions to minimize the damage, and communicated clearly with the client. The project didn't end up being perfect, but it was finished, and I learned from the experience.

As the years went on, the challenges only grew. My business, personal life, and relationships were all tested, sometimes to the breaking point. But through each difficulty, I learned the value of resilience. The key to bouncing back wasn't just in my ability to recover, but in my ability to learn, adapt, and grow from each setback. Life's challenges became stepping-stones rather than roadblocks.

At one of the lowest points in my life, when my marriage ended, I found strength I didn't know I had. I had to rebuild everything from my personal life to my business. But the lessons from construction–the importance of solid foundations, planning, and adaptability–helped me rebuild and recover.

The Need to Bounce Back from Failures

I was young in the above story, driven, and determined to succeed, but I had little experience and often didn't know what I was doing. I didn't listen to advice, I didn't seek help, and I thought I could do everything myself. The result? Mistakes, many of them big ones.

I'll never forget another major setback I encountered. I had launched a new project, eager to prove myself. However, it was a public project, my first large-scale build. Until then, I had only dealt with private clients. Everything changed. I had to deal with public administration, and even the language was different and unfamiliar. The safety regulations, the documentation, the procedures were all new to me. I came from a world where private contracts were sealed with a handshake, rarely written down, and the only point of contact was the owner. With the public sector, there were municipal engineers, public service heads, mayors, councilors, and so on, a whole new world for me.

The project ran over schedule, and the costs spiraled out of control. It felt like everything was crumbling. At that point, I could have thrown in the towel. I could have given up, blamed everyone else, or let the weight of the failure crush me. Instead, I decided to take responsibility. I assessed the situation, took a deep breath, and made adjustments. I learned quickly that failure was just a step in the process, not the end of it. It isn't something to be feared, it's something to learn from.

The financial returns from the project weren't significant, but what I gained in experience was invaluable. From that point on, I became more conscious of how I approached every new venture. I built a better process for evaluating risks, managing expectations, and, most importantly, learning from mistakes. The failures didn't disappear, but I began to see them as opportunities to grow.

Lessons from Failure: Turning a Crisis into Opportunity

During another of my early projects, a client demanded last-minute changes to a home renovation, threatening to cancel the contract if we couldn't deliver within an impossible timeline. My team was already stretched thin, and morale was low. Instead of panicking, I gathered everyone for a quick meeting, listened to their concerns, and reassigned tasks based on each person's strengths. I stayed on-site late into the night, working alongside them to meet the deadline. We delivered the project on time, and the client became one of our biggest advocates, referring us to several new customers. That experience taught me that leadership isn't about having all the answers, it's about creating a space where solutions can emerge, even under pressure.

Staying Flexible: The Key to Adaptability

Just as important as resilience is adaptability. The world is constantly changing, and the construction industry, like any industry, is no different. The market shifts, technology evolves, client needs change, and new challenges arise. To succeed, you have to be able to pivot, adjust, and embrace change rather than fight it.

A key turning point in my journey came when I started to diversify my business. I realized that construction was as much solving problems as it was building structures. Clients didn't just need a house or a building, they needed a solution to their specific challenges, whether that was design, functionality, or even sustainability. So, I began to adapt, expanding my skills to include areas like plumbing, electrical work, and air conditioning. This wasn't just to offer a wider range of services; but to become more adaptable to the needs of the market.

This ability to evolve was critical when the industry changed in ways I hadn't anticipated. The economy fluctuated, and suddenly there was less demand for luxury residential projects. Instead of becoming frustrated, I shifted my focus. I embraced new opportunities, focusing more on commercial projects, renovations, and even sustainable building practices that were gaining popularity. This flexibility allowed me to stay competitive and continue growing, even during tough times.

Developing Emotional Resilience

Building emotional resilience is just as important as building physical strength. The ability to handle stress, manage emotions, and bounce back from setbacks is critical for both personal and professional growth. Resilience isn't something you're born with; it's a skill you develop over time.

For me, the key to emotional resilience was learning how to manage stress effectively. When things got tough, I found that exercising in weight training or long walks helped clear my mind and relieve the pressure. Mental conditioning also became a part of my daily routine. I practiced visualization techniques and positive affirmations, training my mind to stay focused on solutions, not problems.

Another important lesson I learned was the power of perspective. When faced with a setback, instead of viewing it as an obstacle, I started to see it as an opportunity for growth. It's how you frame the situation. When things didn't go as planned, I didn't dwell on the loss; I focused on the lessons learned and how to apply them in the future.

Managing Unforeseen Challenges and Difficult Situations

"In the middle of difficulty lies opportunity." Albert Einstein

In both construction and business, crises are inevitable and often appear when we least expect them. How we respond to these crises determines our success, both in the short and long term. In my experience, every crisis has presented an opportunity to demonstrate resilience, problem-solving, and the ability to adapt. One of the key principles I've learned over the years is that, in the midst of a crisis, staying calm is essential. Panic or knee-jerk reactions only add to the problem. Crisis management is about approaching situations with a clear mind, quickly assessing the facts, and making strategic decisions, even when time is of the essence. These moments shaped a framework I call the *Cycle of Resilience and Adaptability*. It's a process for turning chaos into progress, by combining the will to recover with the skill to pivot.

The Cycle of Resilience and Adaptability: A Framework for Thriving

Step 1: Assess: Take a Step Back

The first principle I follow is to take a moment to pause and assess. In those high-stress moments, the instinct is often to react immediately, but I've learned that it's more effective to take a step back, evaluate the situation, and understand the full scope of the problem. In construction, for example, when materials arrive late, rather than panicking or blaming the supplier, I focus on solutions. How can we adjust the schedule or find temporary alternatives to keep the work moving? By focusing on solutions instead of the problem itself, I can keep the project on track.

This principle can be applied in any field, not just construction. For instance, if your business faces a financial crisis, rather than immediately cutting costs, assess what's really happening. Are there areas where you can improve efficiency? What immediate actions can you take to minimize the impact without compromising the long-term vision? It's about gathering the right information, evaluating the situation from all angles, and not making decisions based purely on emotions.

Step 2: Articulate: Maintain Clear and Transparent Communication

The second principle is to maintain effective communication with all stakeholders involved. Whether it's the team on-site, the client, or external partners such as suppliers or subcontractors, transparent and open communication is essential. Letting everyone know about the situation, discussing the potential impacts, and collectively brainstorming solutions often turns the pressure into a cooperative effort rather than a situation where everyone is pointing fingers.

One key aspect of this communication is ensuring that you're speaking the same language as the people you're working with. This means using industry specific terminology with contractors and suppliers but simplifying complex concepts when speaking to clients or non-technical stakeholders. As the leader, it's your job to ensure that everyone has the information they need to make the right decisions and respond to the crisis in the best possible way.

Step 3: Adapt – Modify the Strategy for the New Reality

Once the situation has been assessed and clear communication has been established, the next step is to adapt your approach. Unexpected challenges demand flexibility and strategic thinking. Rather than clinging to a plan that no longer fits, it's essential to step back and determine what adjustments are necessary to align with the new reality.

In construction, this might mean reorganizing the work schedule, sourcing alternative materials, or reassigning tasks to maintain productivity. In business or personal life, it could involve revising goals, reallocating resources, or adopting new strategies better suited to the current circumstances. The key is to remain proactive rather than reactive.

Adapting doesn't mean compromising your vision; it means refining your approach to ensure you still reach your goal, even if the path differs from what you originally envisioned. The ability to change course and make strategic modifications is what separates those who get stuck from those who move forward.

Step 4: Act – Move Forward with Confidence and Determination

After reassessing the situation, communicating effectively, and adapting the strategy, the final step is to act decisively. Hesitation can create further problems, while confident execution instills trust in your team, clients, and all involved stakeholders.

At this stage, the groundwork is laid: you understand the problem, have identified solutions, and have rallied everyone toward the same direction. Now it's time to put the plan into action with determination. Whether it's pushing forward a delayed project, implementing a new business strategy, or rebuilding after a personal setback, your ability to act with confidence sets the stage for success.

This principle is about trusting in your capacity to navigate adversity. How you handle challenges defines your leadership and earns the respect of those around you. Each crisis you overcome becomes proof of your resilience and your ability to transform obstacles into opportunities.

This cycle carried me through that storm-delayed job and the personal rebuild after divorce. It's a tool for anyone to transform adversity into strength.

The Science Behind It: Why It Works

Resilience and adaptability aren't just gut instincts, they're brain skills. Neuroplasticity lets our minds rewire, learning from failure and change. When I rejigged that storm-hit project, my brain forged new problem-solving paths. Science says this boosts the prefrontal cortex, sharpening our ability to decide and adapt over time.

Psychologists call adaptability 'cognitive flexibility' shifting gears without losing focus. The American Psychological Association found that flexible thinkers thrive in chaos because they pivot effectively. Resilience, tied to emotional regulation, helps us reframe stress as growth. Together, they're a dynamic duo for navigating life's storms.

Real-Life Example: Turning Crises into Opportunities

One of the most challenging moments in my career happened during the construction of a wine cellar on unstable terrain. The site was particularly problematic: it was located right next to a high-traffic road on one side, while on the other side, there were residential buildings with foundations that were far from solid. Before we started the excavation, the client had hired a specialized company to inject cementitious grout into the fragile soil to stabilize it. Given that we needed to dig about four meters deep, this step was crucial.

However, once we began excavation, we quickly realized that the injections had not been done properly. The soil had not been stabilized to the required depth, and there was an imminent risk of collapse. We were already behind schedule, but we could not risk compromising the structure or worse, endangering lives.

Step 1: Assess

This was a high-risk situation which needed immediate action. As soon as the problem became apparent, I ordered an immediate backfill of the excavated area to prevent a collapse and reinforce the adjacent houses.

Step 2: Articulate

I then called the property owner to explain the gravity of the problem. Naturally, he was terrified. But instead of dwelling on fear or frustration, we focused on solutions. Next, I contacted structural engineers to devise a new plan.

Step 3: Adapt

The initial goal was to proceed with the construction of the upper structure while postponing the cellar's completion. This required designing a support system that would allow us to continue working safely above ground while determining the best way to reinforce the foundation before completing the excavation.

Step 4: Act

Over the following weeks, the entire team worked tirelessly to ensure that the upper structure was stable and secure while simultaneously developing a new approach for the cellar. By maintaining clear communication with the owner, engineers, and contractors, we were able to keep the project moving without jeopardizing safety. In the end, through strategic planning, technical expertise, and decisive leadership, we not only salvaged the project but also strengthened relationships with all parties involved.

Building Your Foundation: A Practical Exercise

Want to master this? Try the Resilience and Adaptability Challenge five minutes to tackle any hurdle:

Assess (2 minutes): Jot down a current challenge. What's gone wrong, and how's it hitting you? Example: "A delay's tanking my deadline."

Articulate (5 minutes): How might you word this new path to key stakeholders? Example: "I'll make a call to the client and explain the situation."

Adjust (2 minutes): Brainstorm one fix or detour. Example: "I could rework the timeline or find a backup resource."

Act (1 minute): Pick your move and take one step within 24 hours. Example: "I'll call the new supplier and order the materials."

The Long-Term Impact of Crisis Management

The outcome of this project was not just a successful completion—it also transformed the way I approach crisis management. Once again. I discover that crisis, when handled with care and strategy, can become a turning point in your career and business. The experience reinforced trust between me and my clients. They saw firsthand that I was a leader capable of navigating crises and delivering results, even when the odds were against us.

Moreover, the lessons learned were applied to future projects, allowing me to anticipate and prepare for similar challenges. In essence, the crisis became an opportunity for growth, both for my personal development and for the long-term success of my business. This is the core message of crisis management: with the right approach, every challenge can lead to greater strength, better relationships, and a more resilient business.

The Long-Term Strategy for Handling Crisis

Preparation Is Key: While it's impossible to predict every crisis, having contingency plans in place is critical. For example, in construction, I always ensure that we have backup suppliers or subcontractors lined up in case one fails. In business, it's wise to have a financial cushion or a credit line for emergencies. Preparation helps you respond quickly and effectively when crises arise.

Building Strong Relationships: Crisis management is not just about the technical aspects; it's about human connections. By building strong, trustworthy relationships with clients, suppliers, and partners, you create a network of support when the going gets tough. These relationships can be the difference between failing and thriving when facing challenges.

Learning from Crisis: After the dust settles, it's important to conduct a post-crisis analysis. What went well, and what could have been done better? These lessons should be documented and integrated into your business strategy for future crises. This continuous learning and adapting process turns every crisis into an opportunity for improvement.

Mentorship and Leadership: As a leader, it's your job to guide your team through crises. Be a mentor during tough times by helping your team stay focused on the solution, not the problem. Their confidence in you will bolster the overall resilience of the team, and this can be a pivotal factor in turning a crisis into an opportunity.

Resilience Through Adaptation: The key to thriving in crisis situations is to adapt quickly. Embrace change, seek creative solutions, and adjust your strategies in real time. Adaptation doesn't mean compromising your values or vision, it means finding the most effective way to achieve your goals given the circumstances.

Conclusion: The Power of Resilience and Adaptability

This chapter has been a journey through the challenges I've faced, the mistakes I've made, and the lessons I've learned. Many of those events could have ended in disaster. It's reminded me that success isn't a straight line but a path full of twists, climbs, and descents. And while we can't control everything that happens to us, we can always control how we respond. By keeping a clear mind, communicating effectively, and acting decisively, I found a way forward.

Resilience isn't just getting back up after a fall; it's looking to the future with determination, even when everything seems to be falling apart. It's the willingness to learn from failures, to turn them into building blocks for something stronger. Adaptability, on the other hand, is the art of navigating chaos, of changing course when necessary without losing sight of the goal. Together, these two qualities are the engine that keeps you moving forward, even when the wind is against you.

But resilience isn't built overnight. It's forged in the face of difficulties, in the moments when everything seems to go wrong. It's fueled by small daily victories, by the steps forward you take despite the fatigue. And adaptability isn't just flexibility; it's the ability to see opportunities where others see only problems.

So, as you face your personal or professional storms, remember this: every obstacle is an opportunity to grow. Every failure is a lesson. And every time you get back up, you're building a stronger version of yourself.

Now, take these tools and use them. Face challenges head-on, adjust your plan when needed, and keep building. Because your success isn't defined by what happens to you, but by how you respond. And you have everything you need to turn every storm into an opportunity.

27

Adapting to Thrive

"Success isn't about sticking to a rigid plan; it's about staying flexible enough to navigate the detours and still reach your destination." Mr. Ibba

Success in life and business is rarely a straight path. The most carefully laid plans are bound to encounter unexpected obstacles, delays, and even detours. Change is a constant in every aspect of life, both personal and professional. However, it's not the ability to stick rigidly to a plan that guarantees success, but the ability to remain flexible as your plans evolve. Sometimes it may seem difficult, sometimes even frightening, but it is precisely change that fuels growth, innovation, and the ability to stay competitive.

In the construction industry, no project ever goes exactly as planned. Insufficient materials are delivered, contractors are delayed, or new design challenges arise that require adjustments. External condition change, like new laws or technology. The best builders don't see these as a spanner in the works; they adapt, problem-solve, and find solutions to move forward. The same applies to your personal and professional growth. Being adaptable doesn't mean abandoning your vision or goals; it means adjusting to new information and changing circumstances, while staying focused on the end result. It means embracing change.

Adaptability is not a Weakness

There is nothing wrong when your projects don't go as planned, but a rigid, inflexible approach to your plans can lead to frustration, missed opportunities, or even failure. Adaptability is not a weakness; it's a strength that encourages you to evolve with the times.

An essential aspect of flexibility is recognizing when a change is needed. Often, people resist change out of fear or the comfort of habit. However, acknowledging that something needs to change is the first step in pivoting successfully.

When your plans are met with resistance or unexpected hurdles, rather than viewing this as a setback, consider it as an opportunity to test your resilience and creativity.

The Suffering of Change Is Less Than That of Staying in the Same Situation

Change, though initially frightening, often brings with it a suffering that is paradoxically less than the suffering of staying trapped in a stagnant situation. The fear of leaving our comfort zone may seem overwhelming, but the pain of not evolving, not growing, not challenging ourselves, is far greater. The feeling of being in a place that no longer brings us satisfaction, in a job or an environment that doesn't stimulate our potential, leads to frustration, dissatisfaction, and often a sense of loss.

When I made the decision to move to Australia with my businesses, I had to face a radical change. I enrolled in an English course for six months, a significant step to adapt to a new language and culture. This choice was not easy. I was leaving everything I knew, everything that provided me with security, to embrace a completely different reality. A new culture, new regulations, a different climate, but also new opportunities for growth. Every day was a challenge, but today I can say that the suffering of change was infinitely more bearable than the suffering of staying stuck in a stagnant situation.

Facing change is rarely easy, but it is only through it that we find opportunities to become who we're meant to be.

Real-Life Examples of Adjusting to Challenges and Seizing New Opportunities

I have experienced my fair share of situations where I had to adapt quickly in the face of unexpected circumstances. One example involves a large project I was managing. We were waiting for the roof of a house, and since it was autumn, the forecast predicted rain. The situation was becoming particularly delicate. At that moment, the supplier informed us that due to production issues, the delivery would be delayed by a full 20 days. This would have been a significant problem, as without the roof, the structure would be vulnerable to the elements, especially with rain on the way.

Instead of panicking, we decided to act strategically. We worked with our team and the supplier to find a temporary solution that would allow us to continue work without compromising the structure. We decided to cover the entire structure with waterproof tarps, creating a temporary but secure protection against the impending rain. Thanks to this quick decision, we managed to protect the entire construction and continue work, minimizing damage caused by the weather conditions.

This example highlighted the importance of a flexible attitude and a quick assessment of circumstances. Rather than fighting against the inevitable, we found a solution to keep the project moving. Flexibility allowed us to overcome a significant obstacle without compromising the final outcome.

Navigating Industry Changes

In business, change is inevitable, driven by technological advancements, shifts in consumer behavior, and global economic dynamics. Companies must be ready to adapt, or they risk falling behind. A striking example of adapting to such changes is the e-commerce sector. Just a few years ago, many businesses had only physical stores, but digitalization forced a rapid transition to the web.

Take Amazon, for instance: from a simple online bookstore, it has grown into one of the most influential companies in the world, thanks to its ability to adapt and anticipate trends. Companies that embrace these changes, rather than resist them, can not only survive but thrive.

To navigate change successfully, companies must remain informed, flexible, and open to experimentation. Business leaders must be willing to question the status quo and encourage their teams to think differently and develop new solutions.

Business Evolutions: How to Adapt to New Horizons

In addition to adapting to external circumstances, change within businesses also involves the ability to reinvent themselves internally. A clear example of business evolution is Netflix, which transitioned from a DVD rental service to a streaming giant. This transformation was made possible by the vision of a team that could foresee technological changes and understand audience needs before they became apparent.

Businesses that evolve are those that promote a culture of experimentation and continuous improvement. Leaders must be willing to challenge the existing systems to push their teams to think differently and create innovative solutions.

In business, flexibility translates to an agile approach to project management, adaptive leadership, and the ability to make quick yet thoughtful decisions. For instance, during the pandemic, many companies had to adapt to remote work models. Those that managed to do so without interrupting their operations were the ones that had the necessary flexibility to navigate uncertainty.

Change as an Opportunity for Growth

Change may seem like a threat, but in reality, it is one of the greatest opportunities for growth. Every change brings with it a new chance, whether it's to learn new skills, enter new markets, or create new opportunities. A concrete example is the sustainability movement. Companies that seized the opportunity to invest in eco-friendly solutions, like Tesla in the automotive industry, have gained enormous competitive advantages.

Even on a personal level, change can bring about a "rebirth." Transitioning to a new career, starting a new business, or moving to a new city are all experiences that, although initially difficult, can open new horizons.

Every change comes with the potential to create something new, something better. The key is to view change not as an obstacle but as an opportunity to grow, learn, and improve.

Personal Growth: Embracing Change in Daily Life

On a personal level, change is essential for growth. It can be intimidating, but it is also the key to a fulfilling and meaningful life. Every change brings with it an opportunity to learn, grow, and discover new passions. For example, a professional who decides to transition from a corporate career to entrepreneurship must face many challenges. However, this change can lead to new perspectives, new opportunities, and greater fulfillment.

In my case, moving to Australia was one of the most significant and unexpected changes in my life. Initially, my decision was simple: enroll in an English course for six months, learn the language, and return home. But, as life often does, it changed the course of events. Upon arriving in Australia, I found myself immersed in an entirely different reality. Not just the environment, but the culture, the opportunities, and the challenges were all new.

The Australian culture, open and pragmatic, inspired me to see things from a different perspective. The initial difficulties of adapting, being far from my family and familiar habits, taught me how important it is to face challenges with resilience. At first, I thought I would return to Italy, but as time went on, I began to see new possibilities. The business opportunities were plentiful, and I realized that I could turn my life experience into a successful business journey.

I then decided to move my companies to Australia. It was a bold step, but one I knew was necessary. I had to reinvent myself, rethink my business strategies to adapt to a new market and new regulations. I had to figure out how to integrate myself into a different context, but once I embraced the change, I saw that it was exactly what I needed to grow, both as a person and as an entrepreneur.

How to Keep Your Vision Intact While Being Open to Change

Flexibility in your plans does not mean abandoning your vision or your purpose. It's understanding that the road to success is rarely linear and that the ability to adjust your course, when necessary, will ultimately bring you closer to your destination. Here are a few strategies to ensure your vision stays intact while being willing to adapt:

Clarify Your Core Values: Your vision should always be anchored in your core values. These are the guiding principles that define who you are and what you stand for. When you know your core values, they serve as a compass to guide you even as circumstances change. They allow you to remain steadfast, ensuring that your actions align with what truly matters to you, no matter what external factors influence your journey.

Focus on the "Why," Not Just the "How": Your vision is about the end result your goals and aspirations. The "how" may evolve as you encounter obstacles or new opportunities, but your "why" remains constant. Your path may take you through unexpected detours or straight to your goal, either way, it's the underlying purpose that should guide your decisions.

Be Open to Feedback: Often, the ability to adapt comes from being open to feedback from others. Whether it's from your team, clients, or mentors, feedback is a powerful tool for growth. Use it to adjust your approach, refine your strategies, and uncover opportunities you may have overlooked. Adaptation comes not just from your own observations but from being willing to listen and learn from those around you.

Regularly Reassess: Periodically review your plans to ensure they align with your long-term goals. Don't be afraid to pivot or revise your plans if something isn't working. A successful business or life plan isn't static; it's a living, breathing entity that evolves with time. Regularly evaluate what's working and what's not, and be willing to make the necessary changes to stay on track.

Cultivate a Growth Mindset: A growth mindset is essential for flexibility. Instead of viewing failure or challenges as setbacks, see them as opportunities to learn and grow. By focusing on growth, you allow yourself to change direction, without feeling like you've failed. Embrace mistakes and challenges as valuable learning experiences that bring you closer to your goals.

Set Short-Term Goals with Long-Term Vision in Mind: While your long-term vision should remain constant, you can adjust your short-term goals to better reflect current realities. Setting short-term, actionable goals helps you stay on track, while also giving you the flexibility to pivot if circumstances change. This approach allows you to stay focused on your ultimate vision while remaining adaptable in the face of new information or opportunities.

Conclusion: The Transformative Power of Change

Flexibility in your plans doesn't mean giving up on your vision. The most successful people understand that their vision is the guiding light, but the journey to that vision is full of changes and adjustments that lead you to your destination. Life will throw unexpected challenges and opportunities your way. Don't be afraid to pivot or adjust when necessary. How you respond will determine your success.

Embracing change is the key to staying relevant, innovative, and fulfilled. Whether it's a business or personal transformation, adaptability and flexibility are essential for thriving. Companies that evolve with the market, and individuals who are willing to reinvent themselves and face their fears, can unlock potential and achieve extraordinary milestones.

Change is not something to fear but something to embrace with courage. It is the opportunity to create a better future, to innovate, and to grow. It's never too late to embark on the path of change all it takes is the willingness to take that first step.

Stay grounded in your purpose but remain open to the infinite ways you can achieve it. Adaptability isn't just a strategy; it's a mindset that will serve you well on the road to success.

PART SIX

Expansion and Growth: Building a Solid Business

28

Financial Mastery: Controlling Your Money, Controlling Your Life

"Do not save what is left after spending, but spend what is left after saving." Warren Buffett

Money is a tool, one that can either work for you or against you. Mastering your finances isn't just about making more money; it's about understanding how to manage, grow, and protect it. Without financial mastery, even the most successful businesses and individuals can crumble under mismanagement, poor decisions, or unexpected crises.

The Difference Between Earning and Mastering Money

Many people focus only on earning. They believe that as long as they make enough, everything will be fine. But making money is just the first step. If you don't know how to manage it, it will slip through your fingers, no matter how much you earn.

Think about the people who win the lottery or high-earning professionals who still end up in financial ruin. The problem isn't how much they made, it's how they handled it. True financial success isn't being lucky or making a lot of money; it's making smart decisions consistently.

Keep a Secret Bank Account

No one should know about all of your money. Keep a private bank account where you consistently save and invest a portion of your income. I recommend putting away at least 10% of your earnings into this account. This financial buffer will give you more control over your future, protecting you in case of emergencies or unexpected opportunities.

The Key Pillars of Financial Mastery

Budgeting & Cash Flow Management

Control your money, or it will control you. A budget is a strategy for freedom, not a restraint. If you don't have a clear understanding of your income and expenses, you'll constantly feel financially stressed.

- Know exactly where your money is going.

- Prioritize needs over wants.

- Plan for both expected and unexpected expenses.

- Every business decision should be based on solid numbers. Using accounting software and data analysis tools provides a clear picture of the business's financial health.

A business without financial discipline collapses. A person without financial discipline struggles.

Investing Wisely – Thinking Long-Term

Financial mastery means thinking beyond today. It's easy to fall into the trap of spending as soon as money comes in. But real wealth comes from:

- Investing in assets (real estate, stocks, businesses) that generate future income.

- Understanding the difference between liabilities and assets. Not everything you buy increases in value.

- Reinvesting profits instead of wasting them.

The financially successful don't just work for money, they make money work for them.

Managing Debt – The Silent Killer

Debt is a double-edged sword. Used wisely, it can help you grow (business investments, property, strategic borrowing). Used poorly, it can trap you in financial stress.

- Good debt creates value (business expansion, property investment).

- Bad debt drains resources (credit cards, unnecessary loans, lifestyle inflation).

Many businesses and individuals fail not because they don't make enough money, but because they misuse debt. Learning to control debt before it controls you is a crucial financial skill.

Emergency Planning & Risk Management

No one expects financial disasters, but they happen. Whether in business or personal life, unexpected setbacks (economic downturns, health crises, failed investments) can destroy finances if you aren't prepared.

- Save for emergencies – have a financial cushion for hard times.

- Diversify income streams – don't rely on one source of money.

- Think ahead – anticipate risks and plan accordingly.

Wealth isn't how much you earn but how well you protect what you have. Every business faces risks. Being able to identify them and take steps to mitigate them is essential for long-term sustainability.

Living Below Your Means

One of the most powerful financial habits is learning to live below your means. Just because you can afford something doesn't mean you should buy it.

- If you can afford a $1 million home, buy one for $500,000.

- If you can afford a luxury car, get something more reasonable instead.

- The same applies to clothing, gadgets, and unnecessary luxuries.

This principle allows you to build long-term wealth instead of being trapped in an inflated lifestyle that drains your resources.

Forecasting and Planning

Financial management isn't just about the present financial situation, but also the ability to make accurate forecasts for the future and plan accordingly.

Spend Wisely: Education & Health Are Non-Negotiable

Some people recommend cutting back on food expenses. I disagree. Your body is your most important asset, and you should fuel it with high-quality nutrition. Cheap food leads to poor health, and poor health leads to expensive medical bills and reduced productivity.

Similarly, never cut corners on education. The knowledge you gain will pay you back many times over, helping you make better financial decisions and create more opportunities in life.

From Financial Stress to Financial Freedom

Mastering your finances is about control. When you understand your money, you eliminate stress, make better decisions, and create freedom. The goal isn't just to be rich it's to be financially secure, independent, and in charge of your future.

In life and business, those who master their finances win the long game.

Conclusion: Own Your Money, Own Your Life

Financial mastery is not about luck, high income, or quick wins it's about control, strategy, and discipline. Money can be your greatest ally or your worst enemy, depending on how you manage it. Those who take charge of their finances create stability, security, and opportunity, while those who ignore financial principles live in constant stress, no matter how much they earn.

By budgeting wisely, investing for the future, controlling debt, and living below your means, you create a financial foundation that allows you to thrive. Having a secret financial cushion, prioritizing quality nutrition, and continuing to invest in education ensures that you are always prepared for what life throws at you.

Success is not just about making money it's about keeping it, growing it, and using it wisely. When you control your money, you control your freedom, your opportunities, and ultimately, your life.

29

Finding Your Niche

"The person who follows the crowd will usually not go further than the crowd. The person who walks alone is likely to find themselves in places no one has ever seen before." Albert Einstein

In a world full of competition, finding your niche is not just a luxury, it's a necessity. Whether in business or in life, carving out a unique space where you can thrive is essential for long-term success. The ability to identify a niche that resonates with your passions, skills, and the market's needs will set you apart and ensure you stand out in an increasingly crowded landscape.

The Importance of Carving Out a Unique Space

A niche is your specialized corner of the world, where your unique skills, passions, and experience intersect with the specific needs of a targeted audience. Without a niche, you risk blending in with the mass of a crowded market, competing only on price or convenience

– two strategies that are best for the short term. However, when you have a niche, you create a space where you can offer a unique value that no one else offers. You build authority, trust, and a loyal customer base by speaking directly to the specific needs of your target audience.

One of the biggest mistakes businesses make is trying to be everything to everyone. This approach dilutes their message and scatters their resources too thinly. Focusing on a niche allows you to become an expert in that area, which helps you build credibility and attract clients who value your specialized knowledge.

How I Identified My Niche

In my journey, finding a niche was not a direct or easy process. It took years of trial and error, experimentation, and an unwavering commitment to my craft. When I entered the construction world, I focused on every type of project – residential, commercial, small projects, large projects – trying to get into as many opportunities as possible. But over time, I realized that spreading myself too thin wasn't serving me. The work was vast, but my ability to focus on each type of project with the precision and excellence I aspired to was being compromised.

It wasn't until I took a step back and analyzed my strengths and areas where I could provide the most value that I began to clearly see my niche. I realized I could offer a complete architecture and design experience that included not only the building but also the vision, execution, and lasting impact. This insight became the foundation of my business Florence Homes: offering not just buildings, but high-quality spaces designed to inspire and serve a purpose beyond their walls.

In business, finding your niche means identifying what you can do better than anyone else. It's about aligning your talents and passions with a clear and unmet need in the market. The more specific your niche, the stronger your brand will be.

Steps to Find Your Unique Value Proposition

Finding your niche doesn't happen overnight, but with a clear process, you can get there faster. Here are the steps I followed to identify my niche and how you can apply them to your business or life:

Know Your Strengths and Passions

The first step is to honestly assess your strengths and passions. What are you good at? What excites you? Finding a niche is about using your unique talents. By focusing on what you excel at and what you love doing, you will be able to drill into your specialist area. This creates authenticity in your work and gives you the drive to keep pushing forward. In my case, my background in construction, design, and architecture provided the foundation. But my passion for creating spaces that improve lives, rather than just focusing on the technical aspects, became the driving force behind my niche.

Identify Market Gaps and Needs

Once you know your strengths, look for gaps or unmet areas in the market. What are people struggling with in your industry? What's missing in the market that you could provide? Your niche should address a specific need or solve a problem that no one else is adequately addressing. This requires research, observation, and listening to the pain points of your target audience. For me, the market for high-end residential and commercial projects that combine architecture, design, and construction was booming, but many companies were failing to provide a consistent experience from start to finish. There was a gap in the market for projects that were not only structurally solid but also aesthetically powerful, functional, and transformative. By addressing this gap, I carved out my niche.

Analyze the Competition

You can't carve out a niche without understanding the competition. Research others in your industry who offer similar products or services. What are they doing well? Where are they lacking? How can you differentiate yourself from them? It's not about copying; it's about identifying how you can stand out by offering something better or different. In my business, many construction companies focused on volume, while others focused on design but lacked expertise in the construction process.

I combined both–offering an integrated service that delivered quality, from design to final construction, in a way others didn't.

Define Your Unique Selling Proposition (USP)

Your USP is what sets you apart. It's the promise you make to your audience about the value they will receive. When defining your USP, clarify the specific benefits you provide and why people should choose you over the competition. For my business, the USP was clear: we offered a comprehensive experience in construction and design, focusing on quality, personalized service, and attention to every detail. This USP not only helped us stand out in the market, but also attracted the right clients who resonated with the value we were offering.

Test and Refine Your Niche

Finding your niche is not a one-time event. It requires constant refinement. Test your offerings, listen to your clients, and be willing to make adjustments. Stay flexible and keep an eye on changes in the market, as niches evolve over time. The key is to remain focused on your target audience and continue providing them with value in a way no one else can. Over the years, my niche has evolved with the market, but the fundamental principles of quality, innovation, and comprehensive service have remained constant. By staying true to my niche and continuing to refine my offering based on feedback, we have managed to grow our business and attract loyal clients.

Conclusion: The Niche – Your Space to Shine

Dare to stand out–in life and business! Finding your niche is not just a strategy; it's a declaration of who you are and what you bring to the world. For me, it wasn't about chasing every opportunity; it was about focusing on what I did best: creating spaces that aren't just functional, but inspire.

When I stopped trying to be everything to everyone and honed in on my strengths, combining architecture, design, and construction into one seamless experience. I didn't just find my niche; I found my calling. It became my signature, my way of saying, "This is what I do, and I do it better than anyone else."

A niche is not about being different for the sake of it. It's about being essential. It's about solving a problem so well that people can't imagine going anywhere else. It's about building trust, authority, and a legacy that lasts.

So, take a step back. Look at your strengths, listen to the market, and find that sweet spot where you can shine. Don't follow the crowd. Create your own path. Because in the end, the ones who stand apart are the ones who leave a mark.

30

Scaling and Sustaining Growth

"To scale without losing essence is the art of true greatness."
Marcus Aurelius

As you build your business or life, it's important to scale and sustain that success over time. Growth, when managed properly, should not only expand your influence and reach but also preserve the core values that made you successful in the first place. Scaling requires strategic planning, effective leadership, and an unwavering commitment to quality. The challenge lies in growing without losing what made you successful in the first place.

Doing more of the same but bigger is not scaling. Growth involves finding ways to do things differently by making smart decisions that enable you to handle larger volumes, more complexity, and greater impact. To scale successfully, you need to maintain the same level of excellence that got you to where you are while embracing new methods, technologies, and strategies to expand.

Personal Story

For much of my early journey, I was convinced I was the only important person in my business. I thought I had to carry the weight of every decision and lead every project on my own. In many ways, I believed I was the cornerstone upon which everything revolved. I was proud of it: after all, I had spent years learning the trade, pouring my heart and soul into every detail, building the business from the ground up.

However, this belief came at a very high price. In 2008, I found myself managing 10 active construction sites, working 16-hour days, including Sundays, juggling clients, employees, suppliers, contractors, and more. I was physically and mentally exhausted. I couldn't see the possibility of delegating. For years, I had done everything myself, and I thought no one else could perform tasks with the same precision. But what really made me reflect was the toll this choice was taking on my health and relationships.

My family, who had always been close to me, was suffering from my absence. The more I immersed myself in work, the more distant I became. I realized that, although the business was thriving, my personal life was falling apart. That's when I understood that I couldn't continue like this. I wasn't just neglecting my family; I was neglecting myself.

That realization was a wake-up call. I had to learn to delegate, trust others, and understand that I wasn't the only one who could carry the business forward. I was just one part of a larger machine. If I wanted the business to grow sustainably, I had to build a team that could carry the work with me. The shift from seeing myself as the only leading role to recognizing the importance of those who worked with me was crucial for scaling my business.

Yet another factor limiting me was I'd never had an example in my family of how to grow a business. My grandfather and father had always managed everything on their own, obsessively, without ever delegating anything to anyone. Growing up in such an environment, I always thought that to succeed, you had to do everything yourself, without asking for help. I didn't have role models who showed me how to build a team, distribute responsibilities, or delegate with confidence.

Even though I had employees who had been working with me for 15 years, all reliable professionals, I had never considered the idea of involving them in a structured way within the organization. I saw them as executors, not as integral parts of the company's evolution. I realized it was time for a change. I could no longer grow the business on my own, and I didn't want to. It was time to involve the team, delegate consciously, and allow them to grow along with the business.

As time passed, I began restructuring my approach: I started delegating tasks, creating systems, and selecting people who could take on greater responsibilities. This allowed me to focus on the bigger vision, while also giving more space to myself and my family.

In the end, I had employees who had been working with me for ten years. They were reliable, true professionals who had learned my way of working and my values. I could finally count on them to carry the business forward without having to do everything myself. This change allowed me to grow as an entrepreneur but also to rebuild the personal relationships I had neglected for so long.

It was during this transformative moment that SuperLuce was born. Thanks to the stability and reliability of the team, I had the opportunity to explore new horizons. SuperLuce started as a branch of the business focused on electrical work, an area I had always considered crucial but had neglected until then. Over time, this branch evolved into SuperLuce LED Lighting, a company specializing in the design and production of industrial lighting solutions, which today represents a core pillar of our group.

The success of SuperLuce was made possible by the ability to delegate, grow the team, and apply the same attention to detail and quality that I had learned in the construction industry. It was a true expansion of our business model, built on solid foundations, ready to generate new opportunities and meet the needs of a constantly evolving market.

Success isn't just about expanding your business: it's also about maintaining balance and ensuring that what you're building serves all areas of your life. Scaling is not a short race; it's a journey of resilience, adaptation, and, above all, collaboration.

Understanding Scaling

Scaling refers to the process of increasing your capacity to grow without being hampered by your existing resources. It's about building a framework that allows for expansion while maintaining efficiency and quality.

The Importance of Scaling:

- Increased Revenue: Scaling allows you to increase your revenue without a corresponding increase in costs. This can lead to higher profit margins.

- Market Reach: A scalable business model enables you to reach a larger audience, expanding your market presence and influence.

- Competitive Advantage: Companies that can scale effectively often gain a competitive edge, as they can respond to market demands more swiftly than their less adaptable counterparts.

Identifying Scalable Opportunities:

- Product or Service Expansion: Consider how you can expand your offerings. For example, a fitness coach might start with personal training and then scale by offering online courses, group classes, or fitness products.

- Geographic Expansion: If your business model allows, consider expanding into new markets. This could mean opening new locations or targeting customers in different regions through online platforms.

Strategies for Scaling Your Business or Life While Maintaining Quality

Scaling is a natural progression when your business or life is growing. However, the larger your operation or vision becomes, the more difficult it can be to maintain the same level of quality. The key to successful scaling is ensuring that you don't sacrifice the standards that have been the cornerstone of your success.

Streamline Processes: One of the first steps in scaling is identifying inefficiencies in your current operations. As you grow, what once worked may no longer be the most effective way to operate. By automating repetitive tasks, optimizing workflows, and adopting new technologies, you can scale more efficiently without compromising on quality. Simplifying processes ensures that as you expand, your core systems and operations remain strong.

Focus on Consistency: When scaling, consistency is paramount. Whether it's the quality of your product, the level of service you provide, or the standards you uphold, it's crucial that every aspect of your business or life maintains the same level of excellence. To ensure consistency, you may need to develop more structured systems, processes, and protocols that can be replicated across different teams or locations. Building a brand that people can trust comes from a consistent delivery of quality.

Invest in the Right Tools and Technologies: As you scale, your business needs to evolve alongside new tools and technologies that can help you maintain high-quality standards. Whether it's project management software, advanced tools in your field, or customer relationship management (CRM) systems, investing in technology can streamline your operations, improve productivity, and provide a more consistent customer experience.

Maintain a Strong Focus on Customer Experience: Scaling also means increasing the impact you have on your customers. While expanding your reach, it's essential to ensure that the quality of your customer experience remains exceptional. Whether it's personalized communication, customer service, or post-sale support, ensuring that your customers feel valued is key to sustaining growth.

Build a Strong Team: As you scale, having a reliable and skilled team is essential. Invest in hiring the right talent and fostering a positive company culture that encourages innovation and collaboration. Delegating responsibilities allows you to focus on strategic growth while empowering your team to take ownership of their roles.

Financial Management: Effective financial management is crucial for scaling. Monitor your cash flow, manage expenses, and reinvest profits into growth initiatives. Consider seeking funding options, such as loans or investors, to support your expansion plans while ensuring you maintain control over your business.

The Role of Leadership and Delegation in Scaling

Scaling requires leadership and a willingness to delegate. You cannot do everything yourself as your business or life expands and trying to do so will only limit your growth. Successful scaling is about building a strong team and empowering them to carry the vision forward.

Empower Your Team: As your business grows, you need to trust others with responsibilities and empower them to make decisions. Leaders must focus on building a capable team, training them, and giving them the autonomy to operate effectively. Effective delegation frees up time for you to focus on strategic decisions and areas where you can have the most impact. The more you empower others, the more you can scale while maintaining quality and leadership in your field.

Lead by Example: Great leaders inspire those around them by exemplifying the values they wish to see in their team. As you scale, it's vital that your leadership remains grounded in your vision, values, and work ethic. Lead by example, and your team will follow suit. When your leadership is solid, consistent, and purpose-driven, your team will have the confidence and drive needed to scale alongside you.

Create a Scalable Organizational Structure: As your business expands, your organizational structure needs to evolve to support that growth. This might mean creating new leadership roles, departments, or processes that allow you to manage the growing complexity without losing control. Scaling requires a framework that can support additional team members, operations, and new ventures while ensuring that everything remains efficient and aligned with your core mission.

Effective Communication: Scaling also means communicating effectively with a larger group of people. As your business grows, so does the need for clear, transparent communication. Whether it's with your employees, partners, or customers, clear communication ensures that everyone is aligned and moving toward the same goals. Leaders must continuously foster a culture of communication to prevent misunderstandings and ensure that scaling occurs seamlessly.

Sustaining Growth

While scaling is essential, sustaining that growth is equally important. Here are key strategies to ensure long-term success:

Continuous Improvement: Adopt a mindset of continuous improvement. Regularly assess your processes, products, and services to identify areas for enhancement.

Encourage a culture of innovation within your team, where new ideas are welcomed and tested.

Adapt to Market Changes: Stay attuned to market trends and consumer preferences. The ability to pivot in response to changing demands is crucial for sustaining growth.

Conduct regular market research to understand your audience better and adjust your strategies accordingly.

Maintain Your Core Values: As you scale, it's essential to stay true to your core values and mission. This consistency builds trust with your customers and employees, fostering loyalty and commitment. Communicate your values clearly and ensure that they are reflected in every aspect of your business.

Build Strong Relationships: Networking and building relationships with other businesses, industry leaders, and customers can provide valuable support and opportunities for collaboration. Attend industry events, join professional organizations, and engage with your community to strengthen your network.

How to Set Long-Term Goals for Continued Growth and Success

To scale successfully, it's essential to set long-term goals that not only align with your vision, but also address the evolving needs of your business or life. These long-term goals should be both aspirational and practical, designed to push you to new heights while maintaining the values that got you there.

Build Milestones into Your Long-Term Vision: Breaking down long-term goals into smaller, achievable milestones makes scaling manageable. Whether it's reaching a certain revenue target, expanding into a new market, or launching a new product, milestones serve as checkpoints that allow you to track progress and adjust as necessary. These milestones also give you something to celebrate along the way, which helps maintain motivation and momentum.

Stay Agile: While long-term goals are essential, they must remain flexible. In business, as in life, things change, and sometimes you need to pivot or adjust your goals to reflect new information, opportunities, or challenges. Regularly revisit your goals and be open to modifying them as you gather insights from your experiences.

Focus on Sustainability: While it's tempting to chase rapid growth, long-term success depends on sustainability. Your scaling efforts should focus on building a strong foundation for lasting growth, rather than temporary success. Sustainability means creating processes, practices, and strategies that can maintain quality, profitability, and customer satisfaction over time.

Balance Growth with Well-Being: Growth and success should never come at the expense of your well-being or the well-being of your team. Setting goals that prioritize balance and personal fulfillment alongside business success ensures that your growth is sustainable in every sense of the word. Long-term success is about building a thriving business and life, not just accumulating wealth or status.

Learn from Others: As you scale, it's helpful to learn from others who have gone down a similar path. Look for mentors, peers, and industry leaders who have successfully scaled businesses or achieved long-term success. Their insights, experiences, and advice can help you avoid pitfalls, optimize your strategies, and grow faster.

Conclusion: Building for the Long-Term

Scaling and sustaining growth requires vision, strategy, and the ability to lead with both conviction and flexibility. It's about managing the growth process carefully and intentionally, ensuring that your business or life continues to evolve without losing the essence of what makes it successful. Through leadership, delegation, and a focus on long-term goals, you can scale your efforts while maintaining quality and staying true to your values. As you set your sights on continued growth, remember that success is built for the long haul—not the short sprint.

Scaling is a journey of expansion, evolution, and transformation, and with the right strategies and mindset, you can create something that not only grows but thrives for years to come.

"Do what you must, and the result will follow." Marcus Aurelius

31

Creating a Company Culture: The Foundation of Success

"Culture eats strategy for breakfast." Peter Drucker

I've seen this truth play out in my own life, from the rolling hills of Sardinia to the boardrooms of my businesses. Culture is the soul of success, and in Sardinia, we know a thing or two about soul.

Here, culture is not just a word, it's a way of life. It's the *sos sonadores* playing their *launeddas* at a village festival, the hands kneading dough for *pane carasau*, the laughter around a table during a *sagra*. It's the respect for tradition, the warmth of community, and the unbreakable bonds forged through shared experiences. These are the same principles I've brought into my businesses.

In my companies, culture is not about policies or perks, it's about people. I treat my team like family, because in Sardinia, family is everything. Gathering for grape harvests, sharing the art of sausage-making, or riding motorcycles together under the Mediterranean sun, these moments are not just fun, but we are building trust, respect, and a sense of belonging.

In Sardinia, we have a saying: *"Su connottu esti mellusu de su no connottu"*, meaning the known is better than the unknown. But I say, the known is only the beginning. True culture is about taking the best of what we know, our traditions, our values, our humanity, and blending it with the courage to innovate, to grow, and to create something even greater.

The culture of a company is its heartbeat: it defines how a business operates, how employees feel about their work, and ultimately, how successful the company will be.

Why Company Culture Matters

Many businesses focus solely on profits, projects, and processes but forget about the people driving those results. A weak or toxic culture leads to:

High employee turnover – Talented people leave when they don't feel valued.

Lack of accountability – Without shared values, trust breaks down.

Low productivity and motivation – People work harder when they feel connected to something bigger than just a paycheck.

A strong and positive company culture doesn't just make employees happy; it creates a thriving business that attracts top talent, builds loyalty, and leads to long-term success.

The Pillars of a Strong Company Culture

1. Defining Core Values – The Blueprint of Your Business

Just like a building needs a solid foundation, a business needs clear core values to guide its growth. These values should be more than just words on a website. They should be lived and reinforced every day.

- What do you want your company to represent?

- How should employees treat each other, clients, and their work?

- What principles guide decision-making in difficult situations?

Your values shape your reputation and the people you attract.

2. Leading by Example – Culture Starts at the Top

Leadership defines culture. If a leader is disorganized, negative, or unreliable, the team will reflect those traits. If a leader is disciplined, positive, and hardworking, those qualities will spread throughout the company.

- Be the example you want others to follow – integrity, work ethic, and vision.

- Set the standard – people respect leaders who practice what they preach.

- Stay consistent – culture is only strong if values are upheld daily.

Culture is not what you say; it's what you consistently do.

3. Hiring the Right People – Skills Matter, but Attitude is Everything

A great culture starts with the right people. Many companies hire based only on experience and skills, but the wrong mindset can destroy team dynamics.

- Hire for character first, then skills – skills can be taught, but values and attitude are harder to change.

- Surround yourself with people who share your vision – team members should believe in the mission, not just the paycheck.

- Let go of toxic employees quickly – a bad attitude can poison the entire team.

The people you surround yourself with shape your success. Choose wisely.

4. Encouraging Communication and Transparency

A strong culture is built on trust and open communication. Employees must feel safe to share ideas, ask questions, and express concerns.

- Regular team meetings – create a space for feedback and ideas.

- Encourage honest conversations – problems must be addressed, not ignored.

- Recognize contributions – people stay motivated when they feel valued.

Clear and open communication builds trust and strong relationships.

5. Creating a Sense of Purpose – People Want More Than Just a Job

People want to feel like they are contributing to something meaningful. A company that provides a sense of purpose, not just a paycheck, creates loyalty and passion within its workforce.

- Define your company's mission – why does your work matter?

- Connect employees to the bigger vision – how does their role impact the company and clients?

- Celebrate milestones and progress – people stay engaged when they see real results.

If your actions lack meaning, motivation fades. Find purpose in everything you do.

Conclusion

Culture is not something you build once and forget, it's the fire you keep alive, day after day, in every decision, every interaction, and every moment shared.

So, as you reflect on the culture of your business or your life, ask yourself: Are you building something that will last? Are you creating an environment where people feel seen, heard, and inspired? Are you leading with the heart of a Sardinian shepherd, guiding your flock with care and purpose?

Culture is not just the foundation of success, it's the legacy you leave behind. It's the stories your team will tell, the traditions they'll carry forward, and the impact they'll make in the world. Build it with intention, nurture it with love, and protect it with everything you've got. Because in the end, culture is not just what you do; it's who you are.

PART SEVEN

MEANING AND LEGACY: BUILDING FOR ETERNITY

32

The Role of Continuous Learning

"If you stop learning, you're doomed to repeat the same mistakes. Growth isn't optional, it's the only way to stand tall when everything else falls apart." Mr. Ibba

In a world that spins faster every day, standing still is a death sentence for success. Those who rise above the chaos are the ones who never stop learning. Knowledge isn't a trophy you polish and put on a shelf, it's a living thing, shifting, growing, demanding you keep up or get buried. The greatest builders, leaders, innovators all share one unspoken creed: learning isn't a phase, it's the pulse of a lifetime.

It's a hard fact, but what worked yesterday might crack today, and what stands tall now could collapse tomorrow. Continuous learning isn't a nice-to-have; it's the steel foundation holding up every ounce of growth, progress, and survival. In business, it opens doors you didn't know existed. In life, it's a muscle you build, a habit you hammer into place, day after day, until it's as natural as swinging a hammer or laying a brick.

The Importance of Constantly Updating Skills

When I first gripped a hammer, my world was small; blueprints on a dusty table, sweat on my brow, every ounce of me poured into turning stone into structure. Design and execution were my kingdom, and I ruled it well. For years, I thought those skills were my forever ticket, that being damn good with my hands would carry me through. But one gray morning on a muddy site, it came crashing down as I watched my crew wrestle with a tool I'd sworn by for a decade, while a rival outfit sliced through the same job with a machine I didn't even recognize.

Technology was sprinting, apps buzzing, strategies flipping overnight and my old ways were crumbling like a wall past its prime. I stood there feeling the ground shift beneath me. I realized that I couldn't be the master of one craft and call it done. I had to keep abreast with the new, welcome change, and keep every edge sharp.the wild game of business that holds it all together. If I didn't learn fast, I'd be the relic, not the rival.

Embracing Learning through Books, Courses and Events

Books cracked open my world. Every page was a window into minds sharper than mine, business titans, leadership gurus, strategy masters offering lessons I'd never scrape from a worksite alone. They handed me their mistakes to dodge, their wins to steal, their ideas to spark my own. But reading was just the spark, I needed more.

That's where courses, seminars, workshops, and conferences came in. They turned theories into action, letting me wrestle with ideas in the real world. I'd listen to experts unpack their craft, asking questions and trading war stories with peers. I made connections with people who'd been in the trenches and come out stronger.

Today, we are spoilt for resources. Online courses, webinars, podcasts are all tools at your fingertips, ready to keep you sharp. It's a way of tapping into the hive mind, building a network, a crew of brains that push you further.

My Personal Journey with Books

I still remember the early 90s, a time when entrepreneurship was booming in Italy, with figures like Berlusconi dominating the scene. Back then, I used to buy *Millionaire*, a fascinating magazine that opened my eyes to the world of business, success, and self-improvement. It was in those pages that I first encountered recommendations for books like *The 7 Habits of Highly Effective People* by Stephen R. Covey. That book was a game-changer for me. It sparked my curiosity and set me on a path of continuous learning.

From there, I never stopped. I devoured books on leadership, strategy, and personal growth, each one adding a new layer to my understanding of the world. *Millionaire* was a gateway to a mindset of ambition and possibility. Those early years shaped my approach to learning, teaching me that knowledge can bring about transformation.

And so, my journey continues. Every book I read, every course I take, every event I attend is a step forward, a chance to grow, and a reminder that learning is the ultimate tool for building the life you want.

The Role of Mentorship in Continuous Learning

Books and courses built my base, but mentors laid the beams that held it up. These battle-scarred guides had walked the path I was stumbling down. I'll never forget a rain-soaked day on a site, water hammering my shoulders, when a veteran builder roared over the storm, "You're working like a rookie. Think like a leader!" His words cut deeper than the wind, searing a lesson no manual could touch: resilience isn't taught, it's forged.

A mentor's role is not to spoon-feed answers. They ask questions, pushing you to your limits, spotlighting blind spots and unlocking grit you didn't know you had. They're the rare ones who don't flinch at chaos, handing you clarity to slice through it. Over the years, I leaned on these voices, some formal, some just sharp-eyed peers across a cluttered table to steer me through storms. They drilled me to think harder, plan smarter, never settle. Their scars became my shortcuts, their triumphs my fuel, accelerating me past years of trial and error.

Creating a Personal Growth Plan with the Continuous Learning Framework

I hit a point where random learning wasn't enough. I needed a blueprint. A personal growth plan became my scaffold, turning scattered lessons into a structure I could climb. With all the information out there, you've got to aim with intent, like plotting a build from foundation to roof.

Here's the Continuous Learning Framework I forged:

Explore (Seek the Gaps): Pinpoint where you're weak or the world's shifting – leadership, tech, whatever's outpacing you. For me, it was seeing my crew lag and knowing I had to master new tools.

Engage (Build the Muscle): Pick your tools—books, courses, mentors—and dive in. I grabbed a tech manual, hit a seminar, asked a rival how he worked that damn machine. Act fast, or it's just noise.

Evolve (Raise the Bar): Check your progress, tweak the plan, aim higher. After that site, I didn't stop at one tool. I kept hunting, refining, until my crew ran circles around the rest.

I set hard goals: sharpen my communication, listen like a hawk, fire up my teams. I tackled tech, dug into finance. Each target was as serious as a deadline on a million-dollar job. This framework kept me steady when chaos hit, a compass when I was lost. Like any solid build, it's not set in stone. Keep reviewing, adjusting, keep climbing.

The Power of Lifelong Learning

Lifelong learning isn't just power, it's a revolution. The more you chase it, the more you see: there's no end to what you can grab. Every day's a shot at something new. Failure's a teacher, success a nudge, others' stories a goldmine. It flips your lens from quick wins to the long haul.

Science backs it up: studies say learning keeps your brain plastic, rewiring it to stay sharp as you age. For me, it's more than that – it's resilience in my bones, adaptability in my blood. It's not just about business; it's how I face life's storms, how I bend without breaking.

Continuous Learning Challenge: Build Your Plan

Here's a quick hit to kickstart your learning:

Explore: Write one skill or area you need to grow—tech, leadership, whatever's slipping.

Engage: Pick one resource—a book, a course, a mentor—and find it today.

Evolve: Commit to one step in the next 24 hours: read a chapter, sign up, call them.

After that muddy morning, I scribbled "tech," grabbed a manual, started that night. It's simple, but it works. Build your edge, now.

Conclusion: Staying at the Top of Your Game

Success is a moving target, and you've got to keep swinging to hit it. That gray dawn on the site, rain pelting my back, I learned under a rival's shadow that standing still wasn't an option. The world's a flood of change, and if you don't learn, you drown.

Forge your plan: explore the gaps, engage with grit, evolve every damn day. Never stop the chase. Lifelong learning isn't a choice; it's your hammer, your steel, your way to shape a life without limits.

33

Building Your Image: The Art of Presenting Yourself to Advance in Life and Business

"Your brand is what other people say about you when you're not in the room." Jeff Bezos

The art of presenting oneself is one of the most overlooked but essential skills in both business and personal life. Many people, despite possessing extraordinary talents, remain in the shadows simply because they don't know how to communicate their value to others. Like an architect who designs a magnificent building but neglects its exterior, many people build a solid career but fail to present themselves in a way that the world recognizes. Presentation is not just about appearance; it's an art that includes self-awareness, strategic communication, and the ability to attract attention authentically.

Building an Image: The Importance of Presentation

In the business world, the way we present ourselves can determine our success. A company that doesn't take care of its image, that doesn't know how to tell its mission and values, will hardly receive the recognition it deserves. Similarly, a person who has developed extraordinary skills but doesn't know how to communicate them can easily go unnoticed. Just like a building, the presentation of oneself must be carefully crafted in every detail. It's not enough to have solid preparation or experience; it must be presented in a way that others perceive it as such.

In business, this means being able to tell your story, having a clear vision, and delivering a message that resonates with your audience. Every meeting, every interview, every presentation is an opportunity to "build" a powerful image of yourself, one that doesn't just reflect past successes but projects who we are into the future. Like an architect who thinks about every aspect of a project, our "showcase" must also be designed with care. Image, competence, communication, and vision must be perfectly aligned to generate trust and attract opportunities.

Non-Verbal Language: The Invisible Structure

Non-verbal language is a crucial aspect of presenting oneself in business and in life. Posture, the way we move, our gaze, and even our energy can communicate more than a thousand words. A skilled architect knows that a building is not just a series of bricks and concrete but also the experience it conveys to those who observe it. Similarly, those who master their non-verbal language can project confidence, authority, and competence without the need for excessive words. Knowing how to present yourself through body language and actions is a value that goes beyond mere appearance; it becomes a message communicated continuously.

In business, a firm handshake, an authentic smile, or direct eye contact are all signals that not only improve the presentation but also establish an immediate connection. Knowing how to read and adapt your non-verbal language based on the situation and audience is key to building trust and authority.

The First Impression: The Importance of Aesthetics and "Look"

In the fast-paced world of business, first impressions are critical. The way we present ourselves in the first encounter, through our look and communication, can determine whether our value is recognized or if we remain in the shadows. It's not superficiality; it's strategy. Like a building, if the exterior doesn't attract attention, its internal qualities may go unnoticed. In business, it's essential to be aware of the immediate impact our image can have on others. The art of dressing for success, of strategically managing our presence, does not mean losing authenticity, but rather enhancing who we are to make a difference.

Consider the analogy of an architect who designs a magnificent, solid structure but neglects the aesthetics. If a person in business has exceptional skills, talent, or knowledge but their initial impression is sloppy or lacking, their prospective clients will not have confidence in them.

In both business and life, presentation matters. Just as a beautifully designed building stands out and attracts attention, a well-crafted personal image helps to capture the attention of others and signals that what you offer is worth noticing. It's not about pretending to be someone you're not, but about strategically highlighting your true strengths. When you present yourself in a way that aligns with your goals, values, and expertise, you increase your chances of being seen, heard, and valued in the competitive world around you.

Authenticity: The Foundation of Presentation

An effective presentation must be authentic. A well-designed building can endure for decades, or even centuries, if its foundation is solid. The same principle applies to our personal and professional presentation. If our image is built on anything other than authenticity, it will eventually crumble, losing its credibility and value over time.

In business, authenticity is the key to establishing real, lasting connections. People are naturally drawn to individuals who are genuine, who embrace their true selves and communicate with integrity. Just like an architect who constructs a building with durable materials, we must create a personal foundation that reflects our true values, skills, and purpose. When we present ourselves authentically, we give people something they can trust, a sense that what they see is what they get. This is crucial, as business relationships, whether with clients, partners, or employees, are built on trust. People want to invest in others who are true to themselves, who aren't pretending to be someone they're not.

Authenticity doesn't mean we stop evolving; rather, it means we remain true to our core principles while striving to become better versions of ourselves.

We create a structure that can weather challenges and stand the test of time. Just as a building's foundation is hidden from view, it holds up everything above it. Our authenticity may not always be immediately visible, but it supports and strengthens every interaction we have. It's the invisible but powerful force that helps us connect, influence, and create meaningful relationship.

Conclusion: The Art of Presenting Yourself to Advance in Life and Business

Effective presentation and image are the most powerful tools for success, both in business and in life. It's not just about appearance, but about how we communicate our value and how we create authentic connections with others. Those who are able to do this are the ones who get noticed, create opportunities, and make a difference.

The business world, in particular, is built on connections, people seeking solutions and relationships that need to be nurtured. Those who know how to present themselves can "build" an image that generates trust, respect, and authority, while also adapting their message so that it resonates with the right audience. Like a good architect, it's not enough to build a solid structure: you must also take care of every aesthetic detail, making the building attractive, visible, and useful. In life and business, it's essential to know how to present yourself not just to be seen, but to be appreciated for who you are and the value you can bring to the world.

34

The Art of Giving: Receiving More Than You Give in Business and Life

"Beneficia non in eo quod datur aut quod fit consistunt, sed in ipso dantis aut facientis animo."

"The value of a gift lies not in what is given or done, but in the intention of the giver or doer." Seneca

In a world that often emphasizes individual achievement, the art of giving is a powerful yet often overlooked concept. We often take giving to mean material things, but it can also be our time, our knowledge, our support, and our kindness. What is truly remarkable about the act of giving is how much we receive in return. It's not just a matter of charity or selflessness; giving opens up channels of abundance that often far exceed what we initially offered.

The Power of Giving in Business

In the realm of business, giving can take many forms. It can be the act of offering your expertise, helping a colleague or client without expecting immediate compensation, or supporting a cause that aligns with your values. At first glance, it might seem counterintuitive. After all, business is often about transactions, and the first rule is usually to ensure that you come out ahead. However, businesses that succeed in the long run are often the ones that focus not just on the bottom line but also on the relationships they build, the value they provide, and the good they do in their communities.

Think of the concept of 'value creation'. This is one of the cornerstones of effective business practice. The most successful entrepreneurs and business leaders are those who give more value to their customers and partners than they ask for in return. For example, a company that invests in customer service, that goes above and beyond to ensure customer satisfaction, often gains loyal clients who not only return for more but also refer others. This willingness to give freely – whether through an outstanding product, exceptional service, or by supporting their clients' growth, creates a ripple effect that brings rewards in the form of growth, reputation, and increased profitability.

Similarly, leaders who give generously of their time and wisdom, whether through mentoring, coaching, or simply lending a listening ear, create stronger, more resilient teams. They build trust, inspire loyalty, and develop a culture of collaboration. When a leader is perceived as someone who is not only interested in their own success but also in the success of those around them, the results are often exponential. The energy you put into helping others will return to you, sometimes in ways you least expect.

The Ripple Effect of Giving in Life

In life, the act of giving takes on an even more profound significance. Generosity enriches both the giver and the receiver, fostering deeper connections and a sense of purpose. Whether it's offering emotional support to a friend, sharing your knowledge with someone in need, or simply being there for others in times of hardship, the act of giving opens up pathways to both personal and collective growth.

But there is something even more extraordinary about giving in life—something that goes beyond the immediate results. It's the belief that, in the grand scheme of the universe, what we give returns to us in ways we cannot always predict or understand. When we give selflessly, we open ourselves up to receiving more than we could ever imagine. The universe, in its mysterious and interconnected nature, rewards us in countless ways: opportunities we never thought possible, friendships that come from unexpected places, or a sense of peace and fulfillment that transcends material success.

The Universe Rewards the Giver

The idea that the universe rewards the giver is rooted in the concept of abundance, the belief that there is enough for everyone. When we give freely, without expectation of return, we send out a signal to the universe that we trust in its abundance. And in return, we often find ourselves receiving far more than we ever thought we had to offer.

Consider this: when we give with an open heart, we align ourselves with the flow of life itself. Think of the natural world: rivers that flow, providing water and nourishment to all they encounter. They do not run dry from giving; instead, they remain full, constantly replenishing themselves. The more they flow, the more they receive. The same is true for us. When we give without reservation, we invite the universe to pour blessings back into our lives. This may come in the form of opportunities, growth, personal fulfillment, or unexpected encounters that change the course of our lives.

On the flip side, when we hoard, when we refuse to give, we close ourselves off from the abundant flow of life. We become stagnant, caught in the belief that there isn't enough to go around. But when we step into the practice of giving, we embrace the reality that generosity, whether through our time, our talents, or our resources, generates its own rewards.

The Transformative Power of Giving

When we make the choice to give, we are not only helping others, we are transforming ourselves. Giving teaches us to be selfless, to look beyond our immediate needs and desires, and to see the bigger picture. It encourages us to act with integrity, to offer our true selves, and to build connections based on trust, respect, and mutual support.

In business, giving can transform not only your success but also your outlook on life. You realize that true wealth is not just about accumulating material possessions but about fostering meaningful relationships and contributing to the world around you. It's about creating something that will outlast you, whether it's a business that continues to serve its community or a legacy of kindness and generosity that echoes through the lives of those you've touched.

In life, giving fosters a sense of purpose. It connects us to others, helping us to realize that we are part of something much larger than ourselves. The more we give, the more we understand that we are not just isolated individuals but part of a greater whole. We are threads in the tapestry of life, and every act of kindness, every gesture of love, every moment of selflessness we give adds to the beauty of that tapestry.

Conclusion: Giving as a Path to Abundance

Giving doesn't always have to be grand gestures; sometimes, it's as simple as offering a kind word, a thoughtful gesture, or a listening ear. The act of genuinely caring for others not only improves the lives of those around you but also nurtures your own sense of fulfillment.

In business and life, the more we give, the more we receive, often in ways that far exceed our expectations. In relationships, when we give of ourselves, we foster trust, empathy, and mutual respect. These qualities create the foundation for healthy, supportive connections that benefit everyone involved. When we give freely, we connect to the universal flow of abundance, drawing opportunities, relationships, and fulfillment into our lives. Giving allows us to create lasting impacts, transform our environments, and build a life that is rich not only in material success but in meaning, purpose, and connection.

So, embrace the art of giving. Let it be a cornerstone of your business and life. Understand that what you give to the world, in whatever form, will return to you multiplied and enhanced in ways you cannot yet see. The universe rewards those who give, and through that giving, we receive far more than we ever could have imagined.

35

Building a Legacy

"What we do for ourselves dies with us. What we do for others and the world remains and is immortal." Albert Pike

Every human being wants to leave something behind that lasts longer than their lifetime. A legacy isn't just about passing on wealth or material possessions; it's about leaving behind something that can inspire, impact, and shape the future. In every field, from construction to entrepreneurship, a true legacy endures and continues to make a difference for generations.

When we look back at history, we see the marks of great civilizations that have left us monumental legacies. The ancient Romans were masters at this. They crafted structures, ideas, and systems that still influence us today. They built their empire not just on the strength of their armies but through their vision of what could last forever. From the Colosseum to the complex systems of law and governance, the Romans showed us that lasting legacies come from thinking beyond the present moment. Their influence continues to shape the world we live in today, much like the legacies we can create in our own lives.

The Romans: Builders of an Eternal Legacy

The Romans understood something that few people do today: the true power of building something that lasts. They weren't simply constructing buildings; they were constructing an empire, an idea, a culture, and a way of life that would influence the world for millennia.

Their legacy wasn't in the fleeting victories or the short-lived moments of glory. It was in the systems they created, like roads, aqueducts, architecture, legal frameworks, and the leadership structures that still shape our world today.

Take the Colosseum, for example. It wasn't just a stadium for gladiatorial combat; it was a symbol of Roman engineering, their commitment to grandeur, and their understanding of what it meant to create something monumental. The Romans built for eternity. Their works were designed with the understanding that they were not just building for themselves but for future generations who would live in the world they created.

The Romans also built their legacy through ideas, philosophy, law, governance, and public works that shaped the Western world. Their belief that they were creating something eternal is embedded in the very way they approached their projects. Their roads connected the empire; their legal principles laid the foundation for modern justice; their buildings stood the test of time.

This mindset of building for the long term is something we can apply to our own lives and businesses. When you start thinking about your legacy, remember the Romans. Build not just for today, but for generations. Think about how you want your work, your actions, and your influence to ripple outward, shaping the future long after you've gone.

Envisioning Your Legacy in Life and Business

My journey, like the Romans, has been about building something that endures. I didn't want to create businesses or accumulate wealth alone. I aspired to build systems, values, and structures that will make a difference long after I am gone. I have written a blueprint that others can follow, something that will continue to inspire, guide, and empower others even when I'm no longer here.

How to Build Your Own Legacy

Think Long-Term, Like the Romans: The Roman Empire didn't just build for their time, they built for future generations. They didn't simply want to leave behind impressive structures or victories; they wanted to create systems that would shape the world for millennia. When you think about your legacy, don't think about the short term. Focus on creating something that will endure, something that will still be relevant and impactful far beyond your time.

Create Systems, Not Just Structures: Just like the Romans created legal systems and governance that lasted, think about how you can create lasting systems in your life and business. A legacy isn't what you build today, but creating a framework that can continue to function and grow even after you're gone. Whether it's a business, a mentorship program, or a community initiative, your legacy will be strengthened by the systems you put in place.

Value The Power of Ideas: While the Romans were skilled at making roads and buildings, they were also a culture of ideas. They left a deep imprint on the world through philosophy, governance, and legal frameworks. What ideas will you leave behind? What philosophies will guide others long after you're gone? Think about the principles you want to embed in your work, your community, and your life. Those ideas are your true legacy.

Mentor and Teach Others: The Romans were great builders, but they also taught others to build. They passed on their knowledge, culture, and systems to ensure their empire would continue to thrive. In your journey, remember that your legacy will be enhanced by how you teach, mentor, and guide others. Help others rise to their potential, and your impact will be multiplied.

Leave a Mark Through Service: One of the lasting aspects of the Roman legacy was their sense of duty to others. They built for the people. Similarly, consider how you can serve others in a meaningful way. Whether it's through your work, your values, or your leadership, a legacy built on service to others will stand the test of time.

Create Physical and Emotional Monuments: The Romans built monuments to their glory, but the emotional monuments you build in the lives of others will be the ones that endure. Don't just build for the sake of building but build to make a difference. Create work that touches lives, that solves problems, and that uplifts others.

Conclusion: Build for Eternity

When you're building your life and business, think about the Romans. Think about how they shaped the world through their commitment to building with purpose and for the future. You have the same power within you to leave behind a legacy that transcends time.

Just like the Romans, you can create something that will last. It's not about how much you accumulate, but how much you contribute. It's not about fleeting moments of success, but about creating something meaningful that continues to inspire, impact, and empower for generations to come.

The question is: What will you leave behind? What legacy will you create? Start building today, and remember that the true measure of success is not what you achieve for yourself, but what you leave for others. Build for eternity. Build something that will last forever.

36

The Greatness of Self-Discovery

"Look within. Within is the fountain of good, and it will ever bubble up, if thou wilt ever dig." Marcus Aurelius

My hope is that these pages have been one of self-discovery for you. Self-discovery is one of the most profound and transformative journeys a person can undertake. It is not a destination but a continuous process of uncovering one's true self, understanding deeper motivations, desires, fears, and strengths. Unlike external goals that are set by society or others, self-discovery is driven internally by the desire to understand who we truly are beyond the roles we play, the labels we wear, or the expectations placed on us. The greatness of self-discovery lies in the immense potential it offers for personal growth, empowerment, and the creation of a life that is aligned with our authentic self. As we peel back the layers of our personality, we get closer to who we are at our core, and in doing so, we unlock the power to shape our future and design a life that feels truly fulfilling.

I began to truly rediscover who I was during the most challenging years of my business journey. It was in those difficult moments, when my company faced its most significant setbacks and the weight of responsibility felt overwhelming, that I was forced to confront myself. It was during those times of uncertainty and struggle that I was no longer able to rely on external achievements or societal expectations. Instead, I had to dig deep within to find the strength to keep going. Those tough years became a catalyst for personal growth, and through the struggles, I began to understand more about my true desires, strengths, and limitations. This awakening has been the foundation of my resilience, and it is through these experiences that I was able to build a life aligned with my authentic self.

The Power of Self-Awareness

The first and most significant benefit of self-discovery is the growth of self-awareness. This is the key to making informed decisions, cultivating healthy relationships, and leading a life that reflects who we truly are. When we truly understand ourselves, we become aware of our driving forces – our core desires, fears, and motivations and how they shape our thoughts and actions. Self-awareness enables us to identify what holds us back and provides clarity on the areas where we can improve. It empowers us to break free from unconscious patterns and make choices that align with our values, rather than being mindlessly swayed by fleeting desires or external pressures. This heightened awareness is not only a tool for personal development; it is the foundation upon which all meaningful change is built. With self-awareness, we gain control over our lives and take responsibility for the direction in which we are headed.

Embracing Strengths and Weaknesses

As well as recognizing our strengths; self-discovery involves accepting our weaknesses. Instead of seeing weaknesses as flaws, we can view them as areas for improvement or as a part of our unique individuality. When we accept both our strengths and weaknesses, we foster self-compassion and emotional resilience. It allows us to approach ourselves with kindness and understanding. Embracing our imperfections helps us to thrive in all circumstances, knowing that we are capable of much more than we often give ourselves credit for. This balanced approach enables us to navigate the complexities of life with a sense of peace, knowing we are on a constant path of self-improvement.

Unlocking Hidden Potential

Often, we are unaware of the vast potential within us until we embark on the journey of self-discovery. Many of us carry untapped talents, latent creativity, or hidden passions that we have yet to explore. By seeking a deeper understanding of ourselves, we uncover these dormant qualities. Self-discovery allows us to recognize abilities or interests that have previously gone unnoticed, leading to new opportunities for growth, both personally and professionally. Unlocking hidden potential transforms the way we engage with the world, whether it's pursuing a new career, nurturing a creative project, or building deeper relationships. By embracing these hidden gifts, we step into a more expansive version of ourselves and open up possibilities that we might have never considered before.

Improved Relationships with Others

Self-discovery not only strengthens our relationship with ourselves but also enhances our connections with others. As we become more self-aware, we understand our own needs, values, and boundaries. This insight makes it easier to communicate openly and effectively with those around us. When we know what we want and need, we can express it clearly, leading to healthier interactions. And understanding our own motivations allows us to better empathize with others. We are able to see their struggles and triumphs through a more compassionate lens, recognizing that everyone is on their own journey. Self-discovery teaches us the importance of respecting boundaries and honoring others' experiences, which ultimately fosters deeper, more meaningful connections. By being more self-aware, we are better equipped to support others without judgment, creating relationships based on trust, respect, and mutual growth.

Living Authentically

At the core of self-discovery lies the quest for authenticity. When we understand who we truly are, we can stop pretending to be someone we're not or living a life based on others' expectations. Authenticity brings with it a sense of freedom, a freedom from societal pressures, from the need to conform, and from the fear of judgment. It allows us to live true to our values, passions, and beliefs without being swayed by outside forces. Living authentically is what leads to lasting happiness and contentment. By shedding the layers of expectation and embracing who we truly are, we find fulfillment in the present moment, rather than constantly chasing external validation. Our actions, decisions, and relationships align with our inner truth, creating a sense of inner peace and harmony that is difficult to attain through any other means.

Finding Purpose and Meaning

Perhaps the greatest benefit of self-discovery is the ability to find purpose and meaning in life. As we uncover our true desires, we start to see what truly matters to us. This process reshapes our perspective on life, turning it from a series of random events into a well-charted path toward fulfillment. Finding purpose ignites our passion and gives us the energy and motivation to push forward, no matter what challenges arise.

Conclusion: A Lifelong Journey of Growth

The greatness of self-discovery lies in its power to continuously transform our lives. It is a lifelong journey that offers new insights, challenges, and opportunities at every stage. Self-discovery encourages us to question who we are, what we want, and how we can contribute to the world in a meaningful way. By embracing this journey, we live a life that is grounded in authenticity, self-awareness, and purpose. Each step we take toward understanding ourselves unlocks new possibilities, propelling us toward a future that is not only aligned with our true selves but also filled with fulfillment and joy. Although the path may not always be easy, the rewards of self-discovery are immeasurable, leading us to a life that is more connected, purposeful, and meaningful.

37

Build Your Life, Brick by Brick

"You don't build a life in a day." Mr. Ibba

Every great construction begins with a single brick. Every success, every milestone, every dream achieved is the result of small steps, courageous choices, and unwavering determination. This book has been your construction site, a place where you've found the tools, strategies, and inspiration to build the life you desire.

You've learned that success is not a random event, but the result of clear vision, careful planning, and flawless execution. You've discovered that resilience is your greatest ally, that mistakes are not failures but opportunities to learn and grow. You've understood that true success isn't just what you build outside yourself, but also what you build inside: character, relationships, and meaning.

Now, you have a choice in front of you. You can close this book and return to your routine, or you can decide to take action. You can pick up the hammer, the screwdriver, the level, and start building. Remember: you don't have to do everything at once. Every brick you lay, every small step you take, brings you closer to the life you've imagined.

Your Construction Site is Open

The world needs builders like you. People who refuse to settle for the status quo, who aren't afraid to get their hands dirty, who believe in the power of turning ideas into reality. Whether you're building a business, a career, a family, or simply a better version of yourself, know that your work has value. This book is just the beginning. The real construction happens outside these pages in your everyday life. Every day is an opportunity to lay a new brick, to take a step forward, to move closer to your vision.

One Last Piece of Advice from Builder to Builder

Don't chase perfection. Chase progress. Don't wait for the perfect moment, because it will never come. Start today with what you have, where you are. And remember: every great builder was first and foremost a dreamer. You already have everything you need to achieve your dreams.

So, take your compass, sharpen your tools, and start building. The world is waiting for what you're capable of creating.

Build your life, brick by brick. And remember: the greatest project you'll ever work on is yourself.

11 Keys to Unstoppable Success of the Builder's Mindset

Success isn't a destination—it's a mindset, a way of thinking and acting that drives you forward, no matter the obstacles. It's about having the right tools, the right attitude, and the right foundation to achieve greatness in every aspect of your life. **The Builder's Mindset** is rooted in resilience, vision, and action, and these 11 Keys will help you unlock the potential within you to create an extraordinary life and business.

These keys are not just about achieving success; they're about building something that lasts, something that's built to withstand the test of time. Each one reflects the principles I've learned and applied throughout my journey, and they're the very elements that form the foundation of unstoppable success.

Key 1: Do not let your mind betray you

Your greatest enemy is often the thoughts that limit you. Control your mind, and you'll control your destiny.

Key 2: Give more than you take

True success is measured by the value you add to others, not just by what you accumulate. The more you give, the more you receive in return.

Key 3: Surround yourself with the right people

The people you choose to be around will either lift you up or drag you down. Be intentional with who you let into your life.

Key 4: Train like a warrior

The body and mind are interconnected. Develop physical strength, and your mental resilience will follow.

Key 5: Master discipline through physical pain

Discipline is earned through consistent, intentional effort. Push your limits, endure the discomfort, and let your perseverance become your strength.

Key 6: Develop a killer work ethic

Hard work beats talent when talent doesn't work hard enough. Outwork everyone and focus on what truly matters.

Key 7: Think bigger than you ever thought possible

Your success is limited only by your imagination. Set goals that challenge you and stretch your potential.

Key 8: Be ruthless with your environment

Control your surroundings, and they'll fuel your success. Eliminate distractions, set boundaries, and curate a space that supports your vision.

Key 9: Master the art of communication

Being able to communicate clearly and effectively is a superpower. Master it, and you'll have the ability to influence, lead, and connect with others.

Key 10: Study failures

Failure is not the end—it's the beginning of growth. Learn from mistakes, embrace setbacks, and turn them into stepping stones.

Key 11: Do it for someone, not just for yourself

Success becomes more meaningful when it's built with a purpose. Build your life and business with a larger purpose that extends beyond your own personal gain.

Each of these keys is a piece of the puzzle that makes up the **Builder's Mindset**. They form the bedrock of unshakable success, and when applied with intention, they will help you build the future you desire. It's not just about dreaming, it's about taking action and consistently showing up for your goals, every single day.

The time to start is now. The foundation is ready, and the tools are at your disposal. Now, it's up to you. Take these tools and start building. Define your values. Create systems that work for you. Cultivate habits that push you toward your goals.

Build with intention. Build with discipline. And build something that will stand the test of time. Because your success isn't an accident: it's a choice. And the choice is yours.

About the Author

Ignazio Ibba is a visionary entrepreneur and master builder with a passion for design, craftsmanship, and innovation. From humble beginnings in construction at the age of four to becoming the founder of multiple successful businesses, including Florence Homes Group, SuperLuce, and Ignazio Ibba Eyewear. Ignazio's journey is a testament to resilience, leadership, and the power of a builder's mindset. With expertise in architecture, lighting design, and eyewear, Ignazio approaches every endeavor with creativity, precision, and a focus on building solid foundations for lasting success, transforming challenges into opportunities and redefining industry standards.

Discover the Mr. Ibba Coaching Program – A Tailored Path to Success

The journey you've embarked on in this book is just the beginning of a profound and lasting transformation. If you're ready to take the next step and apply the principles you've learned to unlock your full potential, I invite you to consider my coaching program.

The Mr. Ibba Coaching Program is designed for professionals and entrepreneurs who seek a pragmatic and strategic approach to growth, overcoming everyday challenges, and achieving tangible results. With a focus on leadership, entrepreneurial vision, resilience, and personal development, the program combines proven methodologies with a tailored approach to meet each individual's needs.

If you're ready to embark on a transformational journey and achieve the success you've always aspired to, visit www.mribba.com for more details and discover how I can help you take the next decisive step in your career and life.

Don't let untapped potential define your future. The change you desire is within reach.

www.mribba.com

info@mribba.com